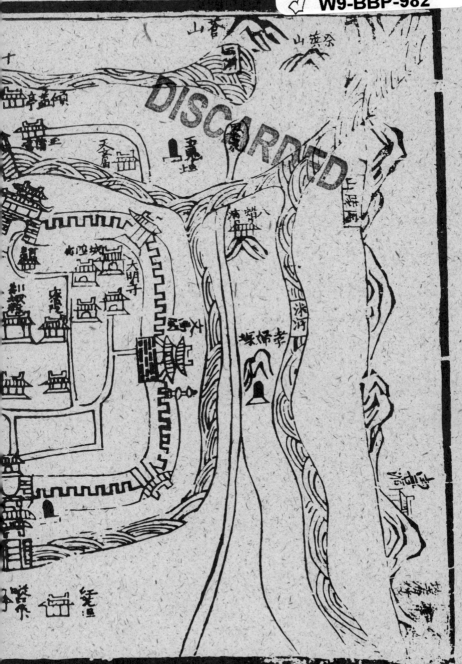

DATE			
APR 0 1 1996			

THE
DEATH
OF
WOMAN
WANG

Jonathan D. Spence

DISCARDED THE
DEATH
OF
WOMAN
WANG

THE VIKING PRESS

New York

First published in 1978 by The Viking Press
625 Madison Avenue, New York, N.Y. 10022

Published simultaneously in Canada by
Penguin Books Canada Limited

LIBRARY OF CONGRESS CATALOGING IN PUBLICATION DATA
Spence, Jonathan D
    The death of woman Wang.
    Bibliography: p.
        1.   Women—China—History.   2.   Runaway wives—
China.   I.   Title.
HQ1767.S63   301.41'2'0951   77–29134
ISBN 0–670–26232–3

Printed in the United States of America
Set in Linotype Fairfield

ACKNOWLEDGMENT
Atheneum Publishers: Excerpt from the poem
"Lost in Translation" from *Divine Comedies*
by James Merrill. Copyright © 1976
by James Merrill. Reprinted by permission.

Front endpaper: General map of T'an-ch'eng County,
from the 1673 edition of *Local History of T'an-ch'eng*

Back endpaper: Layout of the magistrate's yamen
in T'an-ch'eng City, from the 1673 edition of
Local History of T'an-ch'eng

To the memory of my father,
Dermot Gordon Chesson Spence

Lost, is it, buried? One more missing piece?

But nothing's lost. Or else: all is translation
And every bit of us is lost in it . . .

—JAMES MERRILL

Acknowledgments

MY THANKS to many library curators and their staffs for courtesy and prompt assistance: especially to Anthony Marr at Yale, but also to those at the Cambridge University Library, University of Chicago Library, Columbia University Library, Harvard-Yenching Library, School of Oriental and African Studies in London, and the Naikaku Bunko in Tokyo.

Besides the help I received from colleagues and students at Yale, I benefited from audience comments and criticisms when various forms of early ideas for this book were presented in lectures at Harvard (Law School, Anthropology Department, and History Department), at Mount Holyoke, and at Princeton.

I am grateful, too, for much help with translation and interpretation from Parker Po-fei Huang, Andrew Hsieh, and Silas H. L. Wu. All three were generous with their time and knowledge. Thanks also to Anna Maria Insolera and Sally Bozzola, to Ruth Kurzbauer and Florence Thomas, and to Elisabeth Sifton.

Above all, I would have liked to be able to offer my thanks to the late Professor Arthur Wright. This time as always before, but this time for the last time, he had the patience to review countless paragraphs in conversation and to comment on an earlier draft with his critical shrewdness, affection, and vigor. I shall always treasure our last walk, debating woman Wang and T'an-ch'eng county, in the summer night above the sea at Sachem's Head.

Preface

THIS BOOK is set in a small corner of northeastern China during the seventeenth century. The precise location is a county called T'an-ch'eng, in the province of Shantung, and most of the action takes place there in the years between 1668 and 1672. Within that time and place, the focus is on those who lived below the level of the educated elite: farmers, farm workers, and their wives, who had no bureaucratic connections to help them in times of trouble and no strong lineage organizations to fall back on. I observe these people in the contexts of four small crises: the first involved the working of the land and the collecting of taxes from that land; the second, the attempt by a widow to protect her child and her inheritance; the third, the burst of violence that sprang from a local feud; and the fourth, the decision of a woman named Wang, who was unwilling any longer to face an unacceptable present and chose to run away from her T'an-ch'eng home and husband. I say these crises were "small," but that is only true in the context of the overall historical record. To the people actually involved they were of absolute, fatal importance.

I have deliberately tried to keep this story both rural and local, since the accounts that have been written of rural China in the pre-modern period are not based on one local area but assemble evidence across an immense geographical area and over great stretches of time, a process that makes depersonalization almost inevitable. And when local studies have been made, they have tended to focus not on rural areas for their own sakes but rather on areas that had some prior claim to fame: the number of talented men who were born there, for instance; or else the savagery of a rebellion that raged there, the variety and interest of economic conditions, the historical complexities of social organizations. Whereas T'an-ch'eng county was not famous for anything; it produced no eminent men in the seventeenth century, the data on economic and social conditions are scant, and though disasters struck repeatedly the people themselves did not rebel.

It is always hard to conjure up from the past the lives of the poor and the forgotten; and the Chinese thoroughness in the spheres of state and county historiography has ironically been accompanied by the nonpreservation of most local records. One cannot generally find the equivalents of the coroners' inquests, guild proceedings, meticulous land-tenancy records, or the parish registers of births, marriages, and deaths that have enabled such remarkably close and detailed readings to be drawn of Europe in the later Middle Ages. Nevertheless, there is material around, and I have mainly relied on three different sources in my attempt to penetrate a little way into the world of T'an-ch'eng.

The first of these sources is the *Local History of T'an-ch'eng,* compiled in 1673. The county histories of traditional China generally followed a conventional pattern: compiled by members of the educated gentry elite, they treated in ordered sequence such topics of their county's history as its geographical location and topography, its cities and walls, the bureaus and yamens of the local government, temples, the land and tax systems, the biographies of local worthies and incumbent officials (including biographies of women when they were considered to have been of exceptional "loyalty" or "virtue"), and the presence of armies, bandits, or natural catastrophes when these directly affected the county. T'an-ch'eng's *Local History* is not unusual in its content or format, but it is graphic, sometimes vivid, about the county's travails. The intensity of detail in such local histories tends to vary in direct proportion to the distance of a given event from the time of compilation: the 1673 compilation date of the T'an-ch'eng *Local History* means that memories were immediate and harsh for the previous few decades; and the chief editor of the project, Feng K'o-ts'an, seems to have been content to compile an authentically bleak record, not touched up with the brush of nostalgia or propriety.

The second source is a personal memoir and handbook on the office of magistrate compiled in the 1690s by the scholar-official Huang Liu-hung. Again, this is not a totally new genre. There had been such handbooks before, designed to show bureaucrats how to assess their roles and act both in their own interests and in those of their communities. (There was some considerable overlap here, since if a community was goaded enough by the effects of rapacity, stupidity, cruelty, or incompetence to rise in protest or to withhold its taxes, then the magistrate was likely to be heavily fined or dismissed.) The fourteen hundred men serving as magistrates at any one time in the counties of seventeenth-century China were in a difficult position, for though they had enormous power over their jurisdictions, and acted as chief legal officer, financial official, and guardian of public security, they were also the junior members of a complex chain of command that reached above them to the prefects, past the prefects to the provincial governors, and through them to the ministries in Peking and the emperor himself. Furthermore, a finely codified body of administrative law dictated their daily behavior, just as the immense corpus of the *Legal Code of the Ch'ing* developed the precedents of the previous Ming dynasty in attempting to systematize all known kinds of criminal or deviant acts among the population at large and to ascribe fixed punishments for all offenses. The magistrates' interpretations and observances of these laws were subjected to constant scrutiny by their superiors, who also held them responsible for failings of any kind within their local domains. Huang Liu-hung, who served as magistrate of T'an-ch'eng between 1670 and 1672, was no freer from such constraints and pressures than his contemporary incumbents elsewhere. But he was an unusually acute observer, with an eye for detail and an obsession for accuracy: when he wrote his handbook he often gave the precise hour or day (in the cyclical lunar calendar) on which a given event had occurred and the exact sum of money or number and ranks of people engaged in a given transaction or confrontation. When such details can be crosschecked in the *Local History* or other contemporary records, they are exactly corroborated. Huang, therefore, did not content himself with generalizations; in his handbook he illustrated his views on administration and law with individual examples, and it is four of those examples drawn from T'an-ch'eng county that are a central part of this present book.

The third source is the work of the essayist, short-story writer, and dramatist P'u Sung-ling, who lived a little to the north in Tzu-ch'uan county, separated from T'an-ch'eng by a range of bandit-infested hills. Though not well known in the West, P'u Sung-ling was one of China's most gifted and remarkable writers. When I found that he had been writing his stories in Shantung province during the 1670s, and indeed that he passed through T'an-ch'eng in 1670 and 1671, I decided to use his angle of vision to supplement the more conventional historical and administrative writings of Feng K'o- ⬩ ts'an and Huang Liu-hung. For though Feng and Huang take us surprisingly far into the zones of private anger and misery that were so much a part of their community, they were not concerned with penetrating into the realms of loneliness, sensuality, and dreams that were also a part of T'an-ch'eng. Whereas it was just those realms that obsessed P'u Sung-ling, and I have accordingly drawn on him in three of his many dimensions: as a recorder of Shantung memories; as a teller of tales; and as a molder of images, sometimes of astonishing grace or power. It was by combining some of these images in montage form, it seemed to me, that we might break out beyond the other sources from that lost world, and come near to expressing what might have been in the mind of woman Wang as she slept before death.

And so the book ends with woman Wang, as it should, for it is with her that it began. When I came across her story by chance in a library several years ago, she led me to T'an-ch'eng and into the sorrows of its history, into my first encounter with a peripheral county that had lost out in all the observable distributions of wealth, influence, and power. I still do not know how much her story can tell us about the Ch'ing state as a whole, but I would guess there were many women like her, as there must have been many counties like T'an-ch'eng, passively suffering, paying their taxes, yet receiving little in return.

My reactions to woman Wang have been ambiguous and profound. She has been to me like one of those stones that one sees shimmering through the water at low tide and picks up from the waves almost with regret, knowing that in a few moments the colors suffusing the stone will fade and disappear as the stone dries in the sun. But in this case the colors and veins did not fade; rather they grew sharper as they lay in my hand, and now and again I knew it was the stone itself that was passing on warmth to the living flesh that held it.

J.D.S.

Timothy Dwight College
Yale University
May 15, 1977

Contents

✺

THE
DEATH
OF
WOMAN
WANG

One

❁

THE
OBSERVERS

❁

THE EARTHQUAKE struck T'an-ch'eng on July 25, 1668. It was
evening, the moon just rising. There was no warning, save for
a frightening roar that seemed to come from somewhere to the
northwest. The buildings in the city began to shake and the
trees took up a rhythmical swaying, tossing ever more wildly
back and forth until their tips almost touched the ground.
Then came one sharp violent jolt that brought down stretches
of the city walls and battlements, officials' yamens, temples,
and thousands of private homes. Broad fissures opened up
across the streets and underneath the houses, jets of water
spurted up into the air to a height of twenty feet or more, and
streams of water poured down the roads and flooded the irriga-
tion ditches. Those people who tried to remain standing felt as
if their feet were round stones spinning out of control, and
were brought crashing to the ground.

Some, like Li Hsien-yü, fell into the fissures but were
buoyed up on underground streams and able to cling to the
edge; others had their houses sheared in half and survived in

the living quarters as the storage rooms slid into the earth. Some watched helplessly as their families fell away from them: Kao Te-mou had lived in a household of twenty-nine with his consorts, children, relatives, and servants, but only he, one son, and one daughter survived.

As suddenly as it had come the earthquake departed. The ground was still. The water seeped away, leaving the open fissures edged with mud and fine sand. The ruins rested in layers where they had fallen, like giant sets of steps.

It was, wrote Feng K'o-ts'an, who in 1673 compiled the *Local History of T'an-ch'eng,* as if fate were "throwing rocks upon a man who had already fallen in a well." And Feng repeated two general observations that had been made about T'an-ch'eng by a local historian nearly a century before: first, that although one might expect an equal balance between "Catastrophes" and "Blessings" in the chapter of the chronicle devoted to local events, in T'an-ch'eng nine out of ten events fell in the catastrophe category; second, that while nature generally manifested itself in the form of a twelve-year cycle, with six years of abundance and six years of dearth, once in each of those twelve years in T'an-ch'eng there would be a serious famine as well.

Feng lived in T'an-ch'eng county for five years, and life was not kind to him. He came there as magistrate in 1668, but was dismissed after two years for incompetence in handling the finances and horses of the imperial post stations in the county. He stayed on in T'an-ch'eng in deep poverty—ashamed, perhaps, to return to his home in Shao-wu, Fukien, because of his disgrace—and lived on handouts from the local gentry and the money he could get from writing. He was, after all, a *chin-shih,* a holder of the highest literary degree, which he had won in 1651, and there was no one else still alive in T'an-ch'eng with such a degree; there was not even any living native of the county who had gained the lower degree of *chü-jen*. So Feng was honored there and able to make some money by teaching and from occasional jobs, such as being the chief editor for the *Local History*, that came his way. He finished the history by late 1673 and returned to Fukien, but the return brought him only more sorrow. His arrival coincided with the beginning of the Rebellion of the Three Feudatories, and Feng was among the many literati and former officials ordered to take up bureaucratic "office" with the rebel forces. He refused. (In his youth he had refused to read any more of his favorite T'ang poet, Li Po, after he learned that Li Po had written poetry in the entourage of the rebel prince Lin of Yung.) Rather than face reprisals from the rebels, Feng retreated to the Fukien mountains, where the constant exposure in bitter weather led to his death.

Perhaps it was because of his melancholy experiences in T'an-ch'eng that in the brief essays with which he introduced several of the economic sections in the *Local History* Feng wrote so frankly about the miseries of the area, the poverty of its people, and the general inability of the local gentry to help alleviate that misery. He was fascinated by the statistics of disaster in the county, and returned to them again and again: the population of T'an-ch'eng in the early 1670s, he estimated, was only one-quarter of what it had been in the later Ming dynasty fifty years before; where once there had been well over 200,000 people in the county, there now were about 60,000. And the area of cultivated land registered for taxation had dropped by almost two-thirds, from 3.75 million acres to under 1.5 million. His figures grew even more precise as he contemplated the earthquake of 1668, which hit T'an-ch'eng only a few months after he had taken up office there as magistrate, and to emphasize his point he contrasted T'an-ch'eng with its larger northern neighbor I-chou: I-chou county had 108 townships, T'an-ch'eng 45; yet 12,000 people died in I-chou in the earthquake while in T'an-ch'eng (with well under half the population) nearly 9000 people lost their lives.

By 1668 the people of T'an-ch'eng had been suffering for fifty years. Many had died in the White Lotus risings of 1622, when rebels had risen on the tide of local misery in Shantung province, ravaged the cities around T'an-ch'eng, and induced thousands of peasants to leave their homes, by cart or on foot, carrying their few possessions with them. The leaders of the rising, such as Hou Wu, who came from the nearby county of Tsou, offered to the poor a vision of "mountains of gold and mountains of silver, mountains of flour and mountains of rice, fountains of oil and wells full of wine," and promised to all true believers that "for the rest of their lives they would never again be poor." Those who left their homes in search of this paradise eventually died in the mountains, were cut down by government troops, or met their deaths at the hands of other Shantung villagers who fought to keep the roving fugitives away from their own lands.

Many more from T'an-ch'eng died in the 1630s, from hunger, from banditry, from sickness; and in the 1640s a fresh cycle of troubles began. Great swarms of locusts flew into T'an-ch'eng in 1640, destroying what was left of the wheat crop after a summer drought and laying their eggs in the fields; they clung to the walls of the houses and wriggled into people's clothes, they crawled down the chimneys and smothered the fires with their weight when people tried to keep them out by blocking doors and windows. The famine of that winter spread on into the following spring, and groping for words to describe it, the local farmers rationalized their despair in proverb form: "To have the bodies of one's close relations eaten by someone else is not as good as eating them oneself, so as to prolong one's own life for a few days." Or, "It makes more sense to eat one's father, elder brother, or husband so as to preserve one's own life, rather than have the whole family die." Out in the countryside, says the *Local History*, the closest friends no longer dared walk out to the fields together.

Bandits followed in the famine's wake. One such army, several thousand strong, moved down into T'an-ch'eng county from I-chou in April 1641. They looted the market town of Li-chia-chuang, on the county border, and marched southwest to Ma-t'ou market. This they looted too, and spent three days there before setting fire to the shops and homes and moving east to T'an-ch'eng city, which they besieged. But the days the bandits spent in Ma-t'ou had given the people of T'an-ch'eng time to organize their defenses. They blocked the city gates with stones and earth, placed cannon ready for firing on the walls, and marshaled the local defense forces under men like Wang Ying, a veteran soldier who had served the gentry so well in defending T'an-ch'eng during the White Lotus attacks of 1622 that they had petitioned (successfully) to have him named to the official rank of squad commander.

A tablet engraved with the names of 292 men who were among the defenders of T'an-ch'eng in 1641 gives some indication of how the more influential people of the county crowded into the city for safety. The list was headed by two Hsüs, whose lands were in Kuei-ch'ang, to the west, brother and son respectively of a local notable who had won the *chü-jen* literary degree in 1594, and by the scholar Tu Chih-tung, who had obtained the same degree in 1624. The Tus had their lands in Hsia-chuang township, thirty miles northeast, and at least a dozen members of their lineage were listed among the city defenders, as were many from other prominent families—the Changs and the Lius from Kao-ts'e township and the Lis from Ch'ih-t'ou. There were nearly ninety licentiates, or junior degree holders, from all over T'an-ch'eng, perhaps a third of those in the county who held the degree at the time, and a further thirty advanced students who had received the magistrate's certification of competence. There were nearly twenty district and township headmen, who had evidently abandoned the countryside they were meant to be protecting and sought the greater safety of the city; there were junior military officers, physicians, clerical staff from the city offices, yamen runners, merchants, gunnery experts, household servants and—ending the list—one Taoist priest.

This group, and other unnamed citizens, fought off the bandits through the morning of April 15 and finally repulsed them, thanks to some lucky cannon shots that hit the bandit camp and the sudden gusting of a heavy wind that swirled dust and stones around and hindered the attackers. Finally giving up the assault on the main city, the rebels looted its suburbs and then swung south to the post station and township of Hung-hua fou, which lured them with its promise of horses—kept there to serve the routes that ran to central China—and the fame of its brothels. Here the same blinding dust storm had forced the people to take shelter in their homes, with doors tightly closed; unaware of the bandits' approach, they made no attempt to escape, and were cut down in their own homes, or perished when the buildings were set afire. After this raid the bandits moved on to Kiangsu province, returning for three more days in late May, when they wasted a swathe of country around the market town of Hsiachuang.

In such brief and violent raids it was the poor who destroyed the poor, while the gentry were able to shelter behind the walls of T'an-ch'eng city. But there was no place for even the wealthiest to hide when a raiding force of Manchu troops under General Abatai entered the county in January 1643: among the lists of the dead were many who had fought and survived the battle of 1641. In the terse words of the *Local History*:

"It was on 30 January 1643 that the great army invaded

the city, slaughtered the officials, and killed 70 or 80 per cent of the gentry, clerks, and common people; inside the city walls and out they killed tens of thousands, in the streets and the courtyards and the alleys the people all herded together were massacred or wounded, the remnants trampled each other down, and of those fleeing the majority were injured. Until 21 February 1643 the great army pitched its camps in our county borders, south from Shen-ma-chuang along the Shu River, and northwest to I-chou, spanning a distance of seventy *li*** in fifty-four linked camps. They stayed for twenty-two days; over the whole area many were looted and burned, killed and wounded. They also destroyed Ts'ang-shan-pao, killing more than ten thousand men and women there."

In the report that he handed to his ruler after returning to Manchuria, General Abatai did not bother to give details of specific townships. He merely stated that he had obtained, from the general area of northern China:

"12,250 ounces of gold, 2,205,270 ounces of silver, 4440 ounces of precious stones, 52,230 bolts of silk, 13,840 garments of silk or fur, more than 500 sable, fox, panther, and tiger skins, 1160 sets of whole or split horns, 369,000 human prisoners, somewhere over 321,000 camels, horses, mules, cattle, donkeys, and sheep. Besides this is the silver dug up from various hiding places, divided into three parts, of which one part was given to the generals and officers; and the various things which the ordinary soldiers took for themselves, the value of which cannot be calculated."

The Ming dynasty collapsed in 1644, as Li Tzu-ch'eng's rebel army captured Peking, to be chased out in its turn by the troops of the victorious Manchus, but these events, which loom so large in China's history, barely figure in the record of T'an-ch'eng. The *Local History* states merely that after the fall of Peking "there was great confusion, and local bandits

* A *li* is one-third of a mile.

arose on all sides, burning and killing for several months with none to suppress them, so the people suffered severely." And we are told no more of the moment in 1644 when the victorious Manchu troops, now conquerors of China rather than a marauding party of looters, entered the city of T'an-ch'eng, save for the detail that it was the one still surviving *chü-jen* holder, Tu Chih-tung (whose wife and little son had been killed by the Manchus the year before), who now led the citizens out from behind the walls to make their formal submission.

The Manchu conquest of China, with its promise of a restoration of order and prosperity and an end to the old corruption and inefficiency of the Ming, brought no sharp change of fortune to T'an-ch'eng: the decade between the late 1640s and the late 1650s continued the previous pattern. The I River flooded in 1649, ruining the autumn crops along a great belt of land stretching for fifteen miles below Ma-t'ou market. In the autumn of 1651 the I and the Shu rivers both flooded, pouring so much water across the fields that the newly appointed magistrate had to come by boat to T'an-ch'eng city to take up his office, sailing across the sodden land. The next year both rivers flooded after heavy summer rains that destroyed the millet and kaoliang crops and brought a winter famine; while in 1659 the same rivers flooded in late spring after sixteen days of uninterrupted rain, just as the winter wheat and barley were ready for harvest. The farmers watched helplessly as the sheaves already cut went bobbing off across the waves while the heavy ears of still-standing grain fell water-logged below the surface.

With these natural disasters came yet more bandits—in 1648 bandits from the mountains to the northwest sacked Ma-t'ou market; in 1650 a band driven out of their home base in the western Shantung county of Ko-tse sacked the market of Kuei-ch'ang and laid waste the surrounding area; and in 1651 another large bandit force, driven out of their base to the northwest by government troops, broke through the defenses of T'an-ch'eng city itself and sacked it. The *Local History* has poignant stories about each of the raids: woman Yao, aged seventeen in 1648, cursing the bandits as they dragged her out of her house, still cursing as they cut off her arm and killed her; woman Sun, gathering her dead husband's bones and those of her mother-in-law from the ashes of the home the bandits burned in 1650 and proceeding with the funeral rites as the bandits looked on; Tu Chih-tung, who had survived the wars and sacks of fifteen years, refusing to be carried off for ransom in the 1651 raid, cursing the bandits and being killed in his home. Surviving relatives often could not recognize their own family members among the piles of the dead, but would identify them by some item of dress or else reluctantly bury them in group graves.

As Huang Liu-hung found when he came to T'an-ch'eng to serve as magistrate in 1670, the people's problem was one of basic survival—physical and moral—in a world that seemed to be disintegrating before their eyes. When he arrived at his post that summer he asked the locals—both gentry and commoners—about the area, and this is how he recorded their reply:

"T'an-ch'eng is only a tiny area, and it has long been destitute and ravaged. For thirty years now fields have lain under flood water or weeds; we still cannot bear to speak of all the devastation. On top of this came the famine of 1665; and after the earthquake of 1668 not a single ear of grain was harvested, over half the people were dying of starvation, their homes were all destroyed and ten thousand men and women were crushed to death in the ruins. Those who were left orphaned wept with hunger and cold by day, and slept out in the open country by night. Fathers and sons could not help

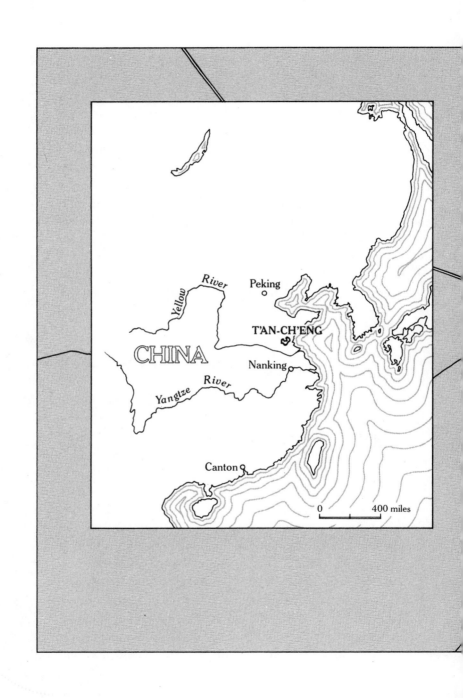

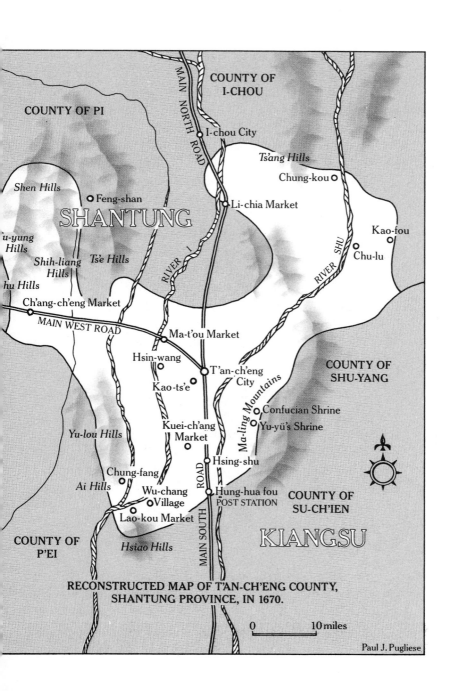

COUNTY OF
I-CHOU

COUNTY OF PI

MAIN NORTH ROAD

I-chou City

Ts'ang Hills

Chung-kou O

Shen Hills

O Feng-shan

Li-chia Market

Kao-fou
O

SHANTUNG

*'u-yung
Hills*

RIVER I

RIVER SHU

Chu-lu
O

*Shih-liang
Hills*

Ts'e Hills

hu Hills

Ch'ang-ch'eng Market

MAIN WEST ROAD

Ma-t'ou Market

Hsin-wang
O

T'an-ch'eng
City

COUNTY OF
SHU-YANG

Kao-ts'e
O

Yu-lou Hills

Kuei-ch'ang
Market
O

Confucian Shrine
O
O Yu-yü's Shrine

Ma-ling Mountains

Hsing-shu

Chung-fang
O O

Ai Hills

Wu-chang
O Village

Hung-hua fou
O POST STATION

COUNTY OF
SU-CH'IEN

Lao-kou Market

MAIN SOUTH ROAD

KIANGSU

COUNTY OF
P'EI

Hsiao Hills

RECONSTRUCTED MAP OF T'AN-CH'ENG COUNTY,
SHANTUNG PROVINCE, IN 1670.

0   10 miles

Paul J. Pugliese

each other, neighbors could not protect each other. The old and the weak moved from ditch to ditch, the young and strong all fled to other areas. Travelers passing through were moved to tears by what they saw, and thought that if this went on much longer no one would be left in T'an-ch'eng."

Over the centuries a certain formalization had developed in China for describing rural suffering; passages similar to this can be found in many local histories and officials' memoirs, and often they may have been mere rhetorical flourishes without substance. But for T'an-ch'eng, at least, the description was real enough. There were twenty-seven county cities in the prefecture of Yen, of which T'an-ch'eng and I-chou were generally considered to be the most impoverished; and when Huang compared those two, he found that T'an-ch'eng was clearly the worse off. There had been eight emergency granaries in the county during the later Ming dynasty: one in each of the four subdistricts of the county, one at Ma-t'ou market, one at the southern post station, one in the county city, and one in the northwestern Shen-shan hills; by 1670 all had been destroyed. The local wealthy who had survived had grown unwilling to make any more donations or to rebuild the storehouses; they did not even respond to a suggestion that they simply lend out grain, for emergency use, to be repaid at a fixed rate of interest by the county until all their capital had been repaid. Similarly, there had been a system of six county schools and three charity schools for advanced candidates preparing for the prefectural examinations, schools endowed with houses that could be rented out to bring in income to pay the teachers' salaries, and with land and kitchen gardens; these, too, were all destroyed or abandoned, and the wealthy had not rebuilt them. They preferred tutoring their sons in their own homes to sharing their resources with the community. The 1668 earthquake destroyed many more city buildings and stretches of the city wall, but even before this many of the buildings were in ruins; the office of the county physician was gone, the bridge that spanned the river on the main road south to Su-ch'ien was down, temples were gutted.

Huang Liu-hung was a scholarly and observant man, from a minor official family in Honan, who had passed the *chü-jen* examination. T'an-ch'eng was his first posting. It was his responsibility to try to hold the shattered community together, and in the personal memoir and handbook that he compiled twenty years later during his comfortable retirement in Soochow, he wrote movingly of his attempts to come to terms with the misery that once surrounded him. It is clear that while he was in office Huang worked skillfully for the community, trying to induce his superiors—and through them the government in Peking—to grant tax concessions and corvée labor rebates, and to be generous in reassessing reclaimed land, so that the effects of decades of catastrophes and the culminating earthquake could be mitigated. To attain such concessions one had to keep constantly pressing, for the government moved slowly, and as far as Peking was concerned, there were hundreds of T'an-ch'engs, each with its own definitions of its own crises, and each one needing to be evaluated on its own terms. Weeks went by before the effects of the 1668 earthquake in central Shantung were examined by officials from the Board of Revenue, and it took eighteen months before tax rebates for the area were approved. The board's final decision was that such an earthquake should be considered in the same light as a serious drought or flood, thus bringing the local population a tax rebate for one year of 30 per cent; this rebate was extended to those who had already paid part of the year's taxes in advance installments. The board also recommended that in view of the high casualties T'an-ch'eng county's assessed labor-service total should be lowered by 400 persons. However, no generosity was seen in this gesture by the local officials in T'an-ch'eng, who estimated that almost 1500 of the earthquake's dead had been on the tax registers as able-bodied males liable for services; the government's decision therefore meant that the local community would still have to come up with 1100 previously unregistered males and draft them onto the corvée labor rolls.

In his reminiscences Huang reflected on the difficulties he encountered in raising morale in the county, for the locals had come to believe that they were caught in a series of crises that robbed their lives of all meaning. "When I was serving in T'an-ch'eng," he wrote, "many people held their lives to be of no value, for the area was so wasted and barren, the common people so poor and had suffered so much, that essentially they knew none of the joys of being alive." Huang observed that this pervasive misery and sense of unworthiness, when coupled with the traditional obstinacy and bellicosity of T'an-ch'eng people, led to stormy family scenes and to a rash of suicides: "A father and son in the same household could be transformed in a moment into violent antagonists; relatives and friends in the same village would get into fights at drinking parties; every day one would hear that someone had hanged himself from a beam and killed himself. Others, at intervals, cut their throats or threw themselves into the river." Huang responded to this by trying to shame the inhabitants of T'an-ch'eng out of committing suicide. In a harsh proclamation that he ordered posted in the rural villages and in the streets of the local market towns, he wrote:

"Those men who commit suicide, hanging themselves from the rafters or throwing themselves into the water, will spend an eternity as ghosts, crammed in the eaves or drifting on the waters. Who is there to pity them if the officials refuse to collect their bodies and leave them as food for the flies and maggots? Those women who kill themselves, dangling from ropes or hanging from their kerchiefs, will haunt deserted alleys and the inner rooms. Why should anyone feel shame if we delay holding an inquest on their corpses and leave their bare bodies exposed for all to see? Your bodies were bequeathed to you by your mothers and fathers who gave birth to you, but you go so far as to destroy those bodies. Only once in ten thousand cosmic cycles can you expect to be reincarnated into human form, yet you treat your bodies as if they were the bodies of pigs and dogs—that is something I hate and detest. If you have no pity on the bodies bequeathed to you, then why should I have pity on the bodies bequeathed to you? If you think of yourselves as pigs and dogs, then why should I not also look upon you as pigs and dogs?"

Despite Huang's words, the world of ghosts and nightmares remained a part of T'an-ch'eng. The *Local History* mentioned how unusually superstitious the people were: over half of them believed in ghosts and magical arts; they venerated women mediums who could conjure up the spirit world as if they were gods; when ill they would never take medicine but consulted the local shamans instead; neighbors would gather in groups and waste thousands of copper coins (which they could not afford) in making offerings as they prayed through the night. One of the most potent local spirits was believed to live in the Ma-ling mountains, just east of the city; he was named "Yu-yü," and Feng had been intrigued enough by this spirit to inquire into its antecedents. He found that Yu-yü was supposed to be a descendant of a Ch'in warrior with an almost identical name who had studied the mysteries of nature and longevity from Taoist sages; when Yu-yü had plumbed all the mysteries of heaven and nature he retired to a cave at Ma-ling, gave up eating the grains of ordinary mortals, subsisting instead on pine-tree wood, on which diet he attained a great age. Also, Confucius's favorite pupil, Tseng-tzu, was believed to have settled in the northwest corner of T'an-ch'eng county, among the Mo-shan hills. The site had been honored with a tablet and a school, though the tablet was now illegible and the school in ruins; local youths, gathering there to play music, would sometimes hear at evening the distant sound of a lute, though no player was to be seen.

Indeed, despite Huang's exhortation, the whole cult of state Confucianism must have seemed remote to most of the people of T'an-ch'eng. Licentiates from the county who had dutifully sat for the *chü-jen* exams in 1669 had pondered three passages chosen that year by the Shantung examiners; they had placed them in their correct context and explicated them. From the Confucian *Analects* there was the phrase "They who know the truth" from Book VI, chapters 17 and 18: "The Master said, 'Man is born for uprightness. If a man lose his uprightness, and yet live, his escape from death is the effect of mere good fortune.' The Master said, *'They who know the truth* are not equal to those who love it, and they who love it are not equal to those who delight in it.'" From the *Doctrine of the Mean* came the phrase "Call him Heaven, how vast is he!" from the closing sentences of Book XXXII, on the man of true sincerity: "Shall this individual have any being or anything beyond himself on which he depends? Call him man in his ideal, how earnest is he! Call him an abyss, how deep is he! *Call him Heaven, how vast is he!"* And from the *Book of Mencius* there was "By viewing the ceremonial ordinances" from Book II, Part I, where Mencius quotes Confucius's disciple Tzu-kung in his absolute praise of his teacher (and of the historian's power): "Tzu-kung said, *'By viewing the ceremonial ordinances* of a prince, we know the character of his government. By hearing his music, we know the character of his virtue. After the lapse of a hundred ages I can arrange, according to their merits, the kings of a hundred ages—not one of them can escape me. From the birth of mankind till now, there has never been another like our master.'" One could dream, from such passages, of how T'an-ch'eng might some day be ruled, or perhaps had once been ruled. But in the event, not a single student from T'an-ch'eng passed the 1669 examination (none had passed since 1646, nor would any pass again until 1708).

In 1670, too, the young Emperor K'ang-hsi issued his celebrated Sixteen Moral Maxims on the maintenance of correct relationships and the avoidance of strife in family and society. Presumably the people of T'an-ch'eng heard the maxims, since the emperor ordered them read in every township and village, but they must have seemed of doubtful utility, and the people often turned instead to their own local variant of the Confucian cult. This variant offered them at least the solace that their city had once had dignity, since it held as its premise the belief that Confucius himself had once traveled to T'an-ch'eng in search of enlightenment. Evidence for this belief could be found in a passage of the Tso-chuan commentary on the *Spring and Autumn Annals,* one of the original Confucian Classics. There it was stated that the little principality of T'an had once existed on the site of the present city, and in the seventeenth year of Duke Ch'ao of Lu (524 B.C. in the Western calendar) the Viscount of T'an had visited the Duke of Lu, where Confucius was then employed. The duke asked why it was that all the senior officials in T'an had once been named after birds. The viscount replied:

"When my ancestor Shao-hao Che came into his inheritance, a phoenix was seen, so to record this bird's appearance he named his officials with birds' names. So-and-so Phoenix was minister of the calendar, so-and-so Swallow was master of the equinoxes, so-and-so Shrike master of the solstices, so-and-so Sparrow master of the seasons' beginnings and so-and-so Golden Pheasant master of their endings; so-and-so Chu Dove was minister of instruction, Tan Dove was minister of war, Shih Dove was minister of works, Shuang Dove was minister of crime, and Hu Dove was minister of public affairs. . . . But after Chuan-hsü came to the throne they could not arrange things by far-off terms and had to arrange them with terms from near at hand; those with offices over the people used terms from the people's world; they could not do otherwise.

"When Confucius heard this he went to see the Viscount of T'an and studied with him. And afterward he said to the people: 'I have heard that when the son of heaven loses good order among his officials, he can learn from the wild tribes around. That indeed seems to be true.'"

The people of T'an-ch'eng claimed to know the exact spot where Confucius had sought the advice of their viscount twenty-two hundred years before—just inside the north gate of the magistrate's current office compound—and the place was honored with a temple, while a more public plaque in front of the yamen announced the general location. Similarly, it was believed that, after his talks with the viscount, Confucius had climbed up into the Ma-ling hills just to the east of T'an-ch'eng, and from that eminence had gazed out to sea; the hill was named after Confucius, and a pavilion in his honor was erected there. Officials may have modified their accounts of these stories with "it is said," or "people believe that," but they themselves covered the sites with their poems, and the shrines were among the first to be rebuilt after the earthquake of 1668. The mountain shrine was adjacent to the spirit cave of Yu-yü, and perhaps each gained prestige from the presence of the other.

Huang Liu-hung accepted them, and let them both be, for they were living shrines. He reserved his censure for the many abandoned temples that were scattered across T'an-ch'eng county and threatened his sense of order. They were natural meeting places for dissolute couples, vagrants, and conspirators, he felt, and should be regularly patrolled or—if possible—boarded up. For to Huang each example of deviant behavior increased the misery of T'an-ch'eng, and the prevalence of lust was clear evidence of the decay of moral fiber. Married women and unmarried girls did not stay within their doors as they should, he charged, but made themselves up and dressed in finery; they strolled by the rivers or rode in fancy carriages up into the hills, where they said they went to worship the gods or pay homage to Buddha; but while there crowds of young people of both sexes mingled together and sported in the monks' lodgings. They were "butterflies besotted by flowers." Huang Liu-hung conjured up more examples of their depravity: young men lounged by the roadside and mocked the women with obscene jokes; the women, swayed by their passions, handed out their enameled hairpins as pledges of their love, behaving no differently from common prostitutes; husbands rented out their wives, servants egged on their masters, old women acted as go-betweens, nuns besmirched their convents, midwives offered other services besides delivery of the new born. The people became like dogs, "running in and out through holes in their back doors."

P'u Sung-ling heard the roar of the 1668 earthquake moving up from the direction of T'an-ch'eng as he was drinking wine with his cousin, by the light of a lamp:

"The table began to rock and the wine cups pitched over; we could hear the sounds of the roof beams and the pillars as they began to snap. The color drained from our faces as we looked at each other. After a few moments we realized it was an earthquake and rushed out of the house. We saw the buildings and homes collapse and, as it were, rise up again, heard the sounds of the walls crashing down, the screams of men and women, a blurred roar as if a caldron were coming to the boil. People were dizzy and could not stay on their feet; they sat on the ground and swayed in unison with the earth. The waters of the river rose up ten feet or more; the cries of roosters, the din of dogs barking filled the city. After an hour or so, calm began to return; and then one could see, out in the streets, undressed men and women standing in groups, excitedly telling of their own experiences, having quite forgotten that they were wearing no clothes."

P'u Sung-ling was born in 1640 and spent most of his life in the town of Tzu-ch'uan, on the northern slope of the mountain massif of central Shantung that bordered T'an-ch'eng in the south. His hometown had been spared the terrors of the Manchu sack of 1643—though not the terrors of anticipation—and he himself can have had little personal recollection of the agonies of the early 1640s; but his stories about the famines of those years, about families of refugees streaming through I-chou on their way south and dying by the roadside, about men captured by bandits ·and sold to the Manchus to work on their estates, about widows struggling to hold onto their lands after their husbands are dead—all have the detailed and authentic ring of tales told by survivors, his townsmen, friends or family:

In 1640 there was a great famine, and there were cases of cannibalism. One day Liu, who was serving as a police runner in Tzu, came across a man and a woman weeping bitterly, and asked them what the trouble was. They replied, "We've been married over a year, but now there is no way we can both survive in this time of famine, so we weep."

A while later he saw the couple again, in front of an oil seller's shop, and there seemed to be some kind of quarrel going on. Liu approached and the shopowner, a certain Ma, explained, "This man and his wife are dying of starvation, every day they come and beg me for a little sesame oil to keep them alive. Now the man is trying to sell me his wife. But in my house there are already more than ten women that I've bought, so what does one more matter to me? If she's cheap, I'll make a deal; if not, that's that! It's really ridiculous that he should go on bothering me like this."

To this the man replied, "Grain now costs as much as pearls; unless I can get at least three hundred cash I won't have enough to pay to run away somewhere else. Obviously both of us want to stay alive—if I sell her and even so don't get enough money to escape death, then what have we gained? It is not that I want to be blunt, rather I am just asking you to show me a bit of charity for which you'll be rewarded in the underworld."

Liu was moved by the story, and asked Ma how much he would offer. "In these days the price for a woman is only about one hundred cash," said Ma.

Liu asked him not to bring down the price, and also said that he would be willing to put up half of it, but Ma wouldn't agree; so Liu, who was young and easily upset, said to the man, "He's a mean-spirited person, not worth bothering about. I'd like to make you a present of the sum you mentioned; if you can escape this disaster, and stay together with your wife, won't that be the best thing of all?" So he gave them the sum from his purse; the couple wept in thanks, and departed.

P'u Sung-ling was seven when serious disasters occurred in his hometown. That summer the bandit army of Hsieh Ch'ien managed to seize Tzu-ch'uan and hold out there for over two months, while a Manchu army slowly assembled and prepared to recapture the city. The deaths and suicides of men and women in Tzu-ch'uan during that year of 1647 dominate the Tzu-ch'uan *Local History,* just as those in 1643 did that of T'an-ch'eng; and the occupying army may have been little better than the rebels it came to oust, if we may judge from the preamble of one of P'u's later stories: "Whenever a great army comes to an area," he wrote, "it causes worse destruction than a force of bandits; for if the people catch some of the bandits they can wreak vengeance on them, but the people do not dare take vengeance against soldiers. The one way troops differ slightly from bandits is that they do not dare to kill people quite so heedlessly."

P'u was also powerfully moved by the massive rebellion of Yü Ch'i, which ran to its end in eastern Shantung during November and December 1661. He writes of the mass executions and the mass graves where surviving relatives could not locate their dead to claim them; of the artisans of Chi-nan making modest fortunes out of coffin building until the better qualities of wood ran out; of fugitives hiding, when a detachment of rebels unexpectedly returned, among the piles of corpses; of families who fled to caves in the hills only to be trapped and killed, their possessions burned. And in this and other rebellions he saw the social changes that were generated as class and regional lines blurred among the refugees: how gentry turned to lead bandit gangs in self-defense or dreamed briefly of personal triumphs, how a literatus could marry a bandit's daughter under compulsion but come to love her as a wife. He writes of robbers who claimed they only killed "unrighteous men"; of a destitute married couple carefully discussing whether the man should become a bandit or the woman a prostitute; of a Shantung gang that burned the feet of the members of a wealthy family to force them to say where their wealth was hidden, and then left the family's private granary open so that the starving poor of the village could loot it at their leisure.

Throughout this period the mountains that lay between Tzu-ch'uan and T'an-ch'eng were a base for bandits, who could strike out to the north or south at the comparatively defenseless townships in the valleys. Both T'eng and I counties, west of T'an-ch'eng, were notorious for their troublesome gangs, which had become a byword in other local histories. P'u described the situation sardonically in one of his briefest stories:

"During the Shun-chih reign,* in the counties of T'eng and I, seven out of every ten people were rebels, and the officials did not dare arrest them all. Later, when things were settled, the magistrates classified them separately as 'rebel households.' Whenever there was a conflict between these households and the good local people, the magistrates used to slant their decisions in favor of the rebels, fearing that otherwise they might rebel again. So it came about that litigants would falsely claim to be 'rebel households' and their opponents would struggle to prove the claim invalid: both claims would have to be laid out, and before one could decide the rights and wrongs of the case one had to decide if the claim to be a rebel was true or false; back and forth went the arguments and counterarguments, and much time was spent checking out the registries.

"It happened that in one of the magistrate's yamens there were a great many fox spirits, and since they bewitched the magistrate's daughter, he sent for a shaman; this latter, by means of a spell, trapped the fox spirits in a bottle, which he then threw into the fire. At which one of the foxes in the bottle shouted out, 'But I am from a rebel household.' None of those who heard this could hold back his laughter."

In many of P'u Sung-ling's stories fantasy and reality are fused in this way, as he struggled to define the inexpressible world in which he had grown up. For he was deeply interested in such local beliefs, and varied between mocking some as superstitious and taking others seriously. He was particularly intrigued by ventriloquy, which was something of a Shantung specialty, and described how one Shantung medium—skilled at this art—plied her trade:

"One day a woman of twenty-four or twenty-five came to my village; she carried a bagful of remedies and offered to sell her medical art. When someone sought advice about their

* The first Ch'ing emperor, who ruled from 1644 to 1661.

illness, the young woman replied that she could not supply
the prescription herself but that she would have to wait until
darkness to consult the spirits. That evening she cleaned out a
little room and shut herself inside. A crowd of people pressed
around the door and windows, ears ready for any sound, waiting. There were a few furtive mutterings, but no one dared so
much as cough; inside the room and out there was no move-
ment. As darkness fell, suddenly they heard the sound of the
hanging screen being moved, and the woman inside asked, 'Is
that you, Chiu-ku?'

"A woman's voice replied, 'I have come.'

"The woman also asked, 'Is La-mei with you?' and it
sounded as if a servant girl answered, 'Yes, I've come.' . . .

"After a while they heard Chiu-ku call for writing implements, and then the sound of a piece of paper being torn to
size, the tinkle of the cap as it was removed from the brush
tip, the sound of the inkstick being rubbed across the ink-
stone. Later came the sharp sound of the brush being thrown
down on a table, followed by the soft sounds of little pinches
of medicinal drugs being packaged. After another pause the
young woman raised the hanging screen, and called to the
patient to come and get her medicine and the prescription."

P'u adds that the watchful crowd truly believed that spirits
had been present, although the prescription, once tested on
the patient, turned out not to be very efficacious.

On another occasion P'u Sung-ling was staying with a
friend in a Shantung village; the friend falling sick, P'u was
advised to repair to the house of woman Liang, a medium who
could summon up a fox spirit skilled in medicine:

"Liang was a woman of about forty, and looked extremely
wary, as if she were a fox herself; we entered her house and
found ourselves in a room divided down the middle by a red
curtain. Peeping behind the curtain, I saw a picture of Kuan-
yin hanging on the wall and two or three scrolls of a horseman

holding a spear, with a numerous retinue behind him. At the
foot of the north wall was a table with a little chair on it—not
more than a foot high—and on the chair an embroidered
cushion. It was here, she said, that the spirit sat whenever he
came. We all burned incense and bowed; the woman clapped
three times on the chiming stones and murmured some indis-
tinct sentences. After she had finished this invocation she
courteously invited us to be seated on a couch in the outer
room, while she stood by the screen and tidied her hair; then,
resting her chin in her hands, she told us all the miraculous
doings of the spirit. . . . Scarcely had she finished speaking
when we heard the faintest of rustling sounds in the room, as
of bats calling in their flight; and while we strained to hear,
there was a sudden violent noise from the table, as if someone
had dropped a heavy stone. 'You'll scare people to death!' said
the woman, turning around, and we heard someone sighing
and muttering on the table—it sounded like the voice of a still
vigorous old man. The woman hid the little chair from view
with a palm-leaf fan, and from the chair came a strong voice,
saying, 'Fate unites us, fate unites us.' "

P'u's life at this time was sorrowful, after proud beginnings: he attained the lower literary degree of licentiate com-
mendably early, when he was eighteen, and won the praises
of local literati and officials, but he could never transmute this
into success at the *chü-jen* examinations, the essential next
stage on the ladder to bureaucratic office and fortune. All his
life, as his erudition grew, he relentlessly pursued a higher
literary degree, but the prize always eluded him, and was
granted—with honorific irony—only by special grace when he
was seventy-one.

He found some solace, as he tells us gently, in his children
and in his wife's character and patient loyalty:

"When our eldest son Jo was born, my wife used to take
him by the hand and they'd go and hide near the paths where

they had seen weasels or squirrels—and were thrilled if they could hear them patter by. If the rain hissed down in the yard, if the winds wailed, if the thunder crashed and rumbled, if the chickens screeched out in fear when a wild dog broke into their pen at night, making the pigs squeal and rush around their sty—our son knew no fear, for he had long been sleeping soundly while she gathered the coals into a glowing pile and quietly waited for dawn. . . .

"When she was young she worked hard at her spinning, and even when she was old and had bad pains in her arms she kept on spinning. Our clothes were washed again and again, and even the smallest rents were patched. Unless guests were expected, there was no meat in our kitchen. If I had to go on a journey somewhere, and she got hold of some delicacies, she wouldn't eat them herself but would store them away, waiting for my return. They had always gone bad by the time I got back home."

The irony of this last sentence was real, for the moments of happiness within his own family were constantly being ruined by squabbles between his mother and his sisters-in-law, and by the genteel poverty into which all of them had lapsed after his father's failures· in both the careers he had pursued, the scholarly and the commercial.

It was during this decade of the 1670s, while P'u waited at home for employment or worked drudgingly with local gentry families as scribe or teacher, that he wrote his astonishing collection of stories and notes known as *Liao-chai chih-i*, roughly translatable as *Strange Stories Written in the Liao Studio*. We know from P'u's own account that he drew these stories from a wide range of sources: from his imagination, from earlier collections, from his friends, from acquaintances he met on his travels, and from a growing circle of correspondents. From his own comments in his stories we know too that many were colored by his childhood experiences in Shantung, aided by the recollections of his own relatives. According to the preface he appended to the collection when he was thirty-nine, the work came hard to him, and he wrote in loneliness:

"I am here alone in the night, the light flickers as the lamp burns down; the wind sighs through my bleak studio, my work table has an icy chill. I am collecting scraps of stuff to make my robe of stories, in the wild hope of adding new chapters to the *Tales of the Underworld*. I drink to help the book along but can barely express the force of my bitterness—all I can pass on to the reader is this, but perhaps it will be enough to get me some sympathy. Alas, I am a bird scared of the winter frosts who huddles into the branches that give no shelter; I am an insect in autumn chirping under the moon, pressed against the door of the house in search of warmth. Only those who truly care for me can understand what I am saying."

Yet P'u Sung-ling did not only brood; he could recall himself to himself and recapture the moments when his boyhood and magic had been joined together:

Once, when I was a boy, I went to the prefectural capital at the time of the spring festival. It was the custom there, on the eve of the festival, for the merchants of the different trades to decorate their shops with colored streamers and to parade with drums and wind instruments down to the financial commissioner's yamen; they called this "celebrating the spring," and I went along with some friends to enjoy the fun. On that day the strollers in the streets were packed like walls; on the seats in front of their yamen sat four officials in their robes of red, opposite each other. Since I was just a child, I didn't know what ranks these officials held; my ears were filled with the babble of the crowd's voices and the sound of drums and music.

Suddenly a man leading a young boy whose hair hung loose, and with a carrying pole over his shoulder, climbed up near the officials; it seemed as if he were trying to explain something, but with a myriad of voices crashing like waves I couldn't make out his actual words. I could see that up on the steps the officials were laughing and that one of the yamen attendants called out loudly to the man that he should put on a performance.

"What performance?" asked the man as he rose in response to the order.

The officials conferred together for a bit, and told the attendant to ask the man what he was good at.

"At inverting the order of nature," he replied, and after the attendant reported this back to the officials and they had conferred a little longer, the attendant came back down to the man and told him to produce a peach.

The magician called out to them that he would do it. Taking off his coat, he laid it on top of his boxes, but then pretended to complain to his son, saying, "Our officials have made it impossible for me: the ice has not yet melted from the ground, how is one to get a peach? Yet if I don't get one, I'm afraid their excellencies will all be angry with me."

His son replied, "Father, you've already agreed. How can you get out of it now?"

The magician brooded over this for a long while, and then exclaimed, "I have thought up a good scheme. It's early spring, the snow still on the ground. We'll never find peaches down on this earth. Only in the garden of the Royal Mother Above, where through the four seasons nothing ever fades, may we find some. We'll have to go up to Heaven and steal some."

"How so!" cried the boy. "Do you think there are steps which take one to Heaven?"

"I have my methods," replied the father, and taking from his box a coil of rope that looked to be some forty or fifty feet long, he arranged one of the ends and tossed it away up into the air; the rope stayed there hanging straight down, as if it were caught on something. Then, as he slowly payed out the rope, it rose slowly higher and higher until it merged into the clouds and none of the rope was left in his hands. "Come on, son!" he called. "I'm old and weak, my body is heavy and my joints are stiff; I could never get up there, it must be you who goes." And he gave the end of the rope to the boy, saying, "If you grasp this you'll be able to climb up."

The boy took the rope but looked much put out and complained: "Father, it's you who are confused! How can you expect me, on a rope as thin as this, to climb up to the highest heavens. If it breaks when I am halfway up, what will be left of me?"

But the father urged him forcefully onward: "I've given my word, we can't have regrets now. I urge you to make this trip. It'll be no trouble for you, and when you get back with your loot we'll be sure to get a hundred taels reward, and we'll use the money to get you a beautiful wife." So the boy grasped the rope and went twisting away up it, where his hands had been, his feet followed like a spider on the threads of its web, until at last he reached the clouds and could be seen no more.

After some time had elapsed, a peach—large as a bowl—fell to earth. The magician was delighted and handed it up to the officials; they passed it around to each other and examined it, for a long while unable to tell if it was genuine or not. Suddenly the rope thudded down to the ground, and the magician cried out in fear, "Oh, no! Someone up there has cut our rope. What will happen to my son?" Moments later an object fell to the ground—he peered at it—it was his son's head, he held it in his hands and wept. "The guardians discovered the theft of the peach, they have killed my boy!" And then piece by piece there fell to earth first a foot and then all the other limbs, which the father, plunged in sorrow, gathered up one by one and put away in his box. "I am an old man," said he, "and this was my only son. Each day he came with me on my journeys north and south. Now, because he obeyed his stern father's orders, he has unexpectedly met with this cruel end. I must carry off his body now and bury him." And climbing up to the presence of the officials and kneeling before them, he said to them, "For the sake of this peach you have killed my son. Have pity on me and help me to pay for his funeral, and I will be sure to repay you."

Each of the seated officials, who had watched in horror and amazement, gave him a good sum. The magician took the money and stuffed it into the pockets in his belt. Then he rapped on the box, calling out, "Hey, my little one! Come out and thank everyone for their generosity. What are you waiting for?" Whereupon a boy with tousled hair pushed open the box with his head and came out, turned to the officials and bowed. It was the magician's son!

I have always remembered that strange magic, from that long-ago day until now. Later I was told that followers of the White Lotus Sect could use magic in this way. Were this couple, perhaps, descendants of theirs?

The last sentences may modify the boyhood magic, but in his maturity, P'u Sung-ling could still dream his own dreams and recapture the dreaming of them:

I was once given hospitality in the guest house of subprefect Pi. In his garden the flowers and trees grew luxuriantly; in moments of leisure we would stroll together there, so that I was able to enjoy the beautiful view fully. One day I returned from admiring the garden, feeling terribly tired; I took off my shoes, climbed into bed, and dreamed that two girls, beautifully dressed, came to me with this request: "We have a favor to ask you, and so it is we dare to disturb you thus."

I stood up, startled. "Who is it that wants to see me?"

They replied, "The Goddess of the Flowers."

In my confusion I couldn't grasp exactly what they were saying, but I left the room and followed them. Soon before us appeared halls and courts that reached up into the clouds; at their foot were steps of stone, rising tier on tier; we must have mounted more than a hundred steps before we reached the upper level. I saw a red door, opened wide, and two or three more girls, who went ahead to announce that a guest had come. Shortly thereafter we stood outside a hall. The door fastenings were of gold and the screens of green, their shimmering pierced the eye. A girl came down the steps from inside the hall, the ornaments tinkled at her belt, she looked like an imperial consort.

Before I could pay my respects to her, she anticipated me by saying, "Having respectfully troubled you, sir, to come here, it is I who should be the first to thank you," and she called to her attendants to lay a mat upon the ground as if she intended to pay me obeisance.

I felt myself confused and was unsure how to act, so I addressed her in these words: "I am only a worthless fellow, and have been more than enough honored by the fact that you summoned me here; how could I dare to accept your homage, it would quite spoil my joy."

So she ordered them to take up the mat and set out a feast; we sat to eat facing each other. After we had drunk several cups of wine, I said to her, "I get drunk after drinking very little, and am afraid of acting improperly. If you would tell me why you summoned me, I would feel much more at ease."

She gave me no answer but made me drink another large cup of wine. Again and again I asked her the cause of my summons, until at last she replied, "I am the Goddess of Flowers. The members of my family are delicate and we all make our home here. But often the Wind sends his minions here and they do us great damage. Now I have decided to offer the Wind direct battle, and summoned you to draft my challenge."

I was alarmed and answered, "My learning is so limited that I am afraid of displeasing you, but since you honor me with your command, I will struggle for you with my meager abilities." She was happy at this and took me up into the hall and gave me the necessaries for writing. All the ladies busied themselves, to wipe the table and dust my seat, grind the ink and moisten the brush. One young girl, with her hair dangling down, folded over the paper for me, holding it steady beneath my wrist. I had barely written one or two sentences when the women pressed forward to read it over my shoulder. And I, who usually write so slowly, this one time felt my thoughts pour forth like the rushing waves.

Soon the draft was finished, and the ladies hurried to show it to their mistress. She looked it through and said that it was flawless, at which they escorted me back to my home. I awoke and remembered the details of the scene with great clarity; but of the words I had written, well over half had drifted away.

So as not to lose the stories that came his way, P'u would try to transcribe them immediately; often, too, he would describe their exact provenance, as if to impress posterity with his conscientiousness. Thus in the only case of a story that is set identifiably in T'an-ch'eng, he tells us that he was shown a complete written version of the tale by a scholar in I-chou city as he, P'u, sheltered at an inn there one rainy day, on his way to the south, in the autumn of 1670. The story is about a man of some culture who lives in the post-station area of Hung-hua fou in the southern part of T'an-ch'eng county and has an affair with two ladies at once. The ladies give themselves to the scholar eagerly (as they do in many of P'u's stories), and both turn out to be spirits, one harmful and one beneficial, who had been doomed to the shadow life of wandering ghosts. After a complex plot involving much magic, death, and rebirth, the ghostly spirits are exorcised, the bones of the original victims laid to rest, and the scholar lives peacefully with both women, now in new and human reincarnations. It is a story of fantasy, sensuality, and insecurity, and as such a fitting commentary on the place and time.

Two

❋

THE
LAND

❋

IN JANUARY 1671 there was an unusually heavy snowfall in
T'an-ch'eng. In most years in Shantung snow was a sign of
good fortune, for it protected the young shoots of the winter
wheat from extreme cold and ensured a sturdy growth in the
spring thaw. It was dryness or cold rain that was a worse
threat, and if snow fell the New Year festival was held with
especial joyfulness. But this year the snow did not stop falling.
Huang Liu-hung, riding out to inspect some land on the
border of T'an-ch'eng and I-chou, found the ice thick on the
rivers, and at times his horse floundered in snow up to its
belly. "There were drifts of ten feet or more on the plains,"
says the *Local History,* "and the snow piled up level with the
roofs of the villages and the tops of the trees. Houses were
completely buried, and many of the poor people had to dig
themselves out with their hands. Small villages were cut off
for several days. Birds, wild hares, plants were frozen to death.
With their seeds gone many people had no alternative but
flight, and one could not count those who froze to death along
the road. Truly it was an unusual catastrophe."

Yet it remained a local catastrophe, not a widespread regional one, and since no major exemptions were given by the central government, the tax collectors had to start making up their 1671 quotas.

At this time, T'an-ch'eng was a small, poor county. An oddly shaped administrative area, it had the bulk of its land in a block some fifteen miles square, and from each side of this two long pincers of land curled up toward the north for twenty-five to thirty miles. The southern area was fertile, the site of T'an-ch'eng city, the county capital, and of Ma-t'ou market, the county's major trading center; these two towns sat close together, between the Shu and I rivers, which flowed straight through the county on their way to join the Yellow River. The land in the two pincers was hilly, mountainous in places, crisscrossed by smaller rivers, and surprisingly inaccessible from the county capital. The fertile valley lands between the pincers, which would have made T'an-ch'eng richer, were in fact registered as part of I-chou, T'an-ch'eng's larger and slightly more prosperous northern neighbor.

T'an-ch'eng was an agricultural county, and little was manufactured there: the *Local History* lists three varieties of cotton and silken cloth as being produced locally, but nothing else. Nor did many goods pass through the county: only Ma-t'ou market had much commercial activity, this by road to all directions except the east—where communications were cut by the long range of the Ma-ling mountains—and north and south along the I River, when there were adequate summer rains to keep up the water levels.

This was the winter wheat and kaoliang area of China, with low precipitation, hot in summer and cold in winter. The crops that grew in T'an-ch'eng along with the wheat and kaoliang staples were millet, soybeans and sesame, turnips and other root vegetables, melons and pumpkins, a variety of edible greens as well as onions and garlic, celery and eggplant.

The fruits that grew were peaches and apricots, plums, pears, and cherries. There were walnuts and chestnuts, and some wild animals and birds that could be trapped and eaten—hare and deer, ducks, quail, pigeons and pheasants. So it was, at least, when times were good and the crops grew.

In these areas of winter crops there was little respite for the farming community, and harvesting was followed by sowing rather than by rest. As soon as the snows had thawed and the winter-wheat shoots planted the previous October were growing sturdily, the laborers gave a first turning to the fallow fields and began to carry the human and animal fertilizer from the homes and farmyards out to the land. In early May the fields were deep ploughed in preparation for kaoliang and millet (with draft animals if there were any, otherwise by teams of men), and the farmers carefully dropped, handful by handful, a mixture of seed, fertilizer, and crushed soybean powder into each furrow, each handful being about one foot apart. They leveled the fields with a heavy wooden harrow, and the soft soil was pressed down with a stone roller—those without a roller tramped on the ground with their feet. After three or four weeks, if the weather was kind, the young plants were some three inches high and had to be carefully thinned out with a hoe; a week beyond this the rows were weeded and earth was tamped around the base of each shoot so that it would stand upright as it grew; this process of weeding and tamping was repeated again and again as the shoots grew. By early June, in other fields, the winter wheat had ripened and was ready for harvest; the stalks were pulled out of the ground by hand, bound in small bundles, and carried to the threshing ground by barrow or on men's backs. After the wheat was in, the cleared fields were lightly ploughed and soybean seeds planted in rows (a simple task that children could do) and then covered by harrow; no fertilizer was used unless there happened to be a surplus, but the beans had to be weeded every few days, and the farmers needed hot weather and summer rains. As the beans grew, the kaoliang and millet came ready for harvesting, and in late August the stalks were pulled out by hand and carried to the threshing ground. Turnips, cabbages, and other vegetables were dried or pickled, and stored. There were no orchards—fruit was picked from individual trees as it ripened. The fields lay fallow through September, and in early October the winter wheat was sown; if the young shoots were visible by the end of October, the chances for next year's crop were good.

Like every other county in seventeenth-century China, T'an-ch'eng had a fixed revenue quota that it had to pay every year to Peking. The bulk of the revenues needed for paying local expenses in the county, and for meeting the quota demands of the central government, was provided in the form of two taxes—one was a tax on the land, the other a tax on certain individual adult males (paid usually with cash, but occasionally with labor service). Since the farmers were almost never able to pay the full amount at one time, the government broke the payment into installments for them, so that they paid according to this schedule:

In the second lunar month of each year	20%
In the third month	10%
In the fourth month	10%
In the fifth month	5%
In the sixth month	5%
In the seventh month	15%
In the eighth month	15%
In the ninth month	10%
In the tenth month	10%

In the three coldest months of winter nothing had to be paid.

In T'an-ch'eng's terms the payment in the second lunar month (mid-March to mid-April in the Western calendar) came when winter had been survived and the spun yarn and other handicrafts had been sold; the late spring taxes would be paid after the winter wheat and barley had been harvested; and the autumn taxes when the kaoliang, soybeans, and millet were in. Relief from taxation was also afforded by the lower rates during the hottest midsummer months between the two harvests.

Each of the nine tax-paying months was further subdivided into two halves of fifteen days each, so that the farmers and collectors had eighteen separate tax periods in every year. A period of five days after the end of each fifteen-day block was designated for the local collectors to track down defaulters; the next five days were set aside for the imposition of penalties.

Such a system could only be made workable by a thorough structure of mutual responsibility and supervision. T'an-ch'eng county was divided into four districts, and each of these districts was subdivided into eight townships. Each of the thirty-two townships of T'an-ch'eng had a township head, appointed for one year or longer by the magistrate, and it was this township head's responsibility to make sure that the smaller units in his jurisdiction—subdivided further into villages, groups of five households, and individual households—paid in their tax quotas on time.

In the fourteenth and fifteenth centuries, during the early years of the Ming dynasty, these local tax-gathering coordinators were often from powerful landlord families themselves and could be expected to bring massive pressure to bear on other delinquent households; the office was regarded as an honorific one, and on occasion the holders were even received in mass audiences by the emperor. By the 1660s, however, during the founding period of the Ch'ing dynasty, the post was no longer so coveted, nor did it have the same honorific connotations, though in T'an-ch'eng county one could still find township heads who were widely respected and well connected. Yü Shun, for example, the son of a licentiate and one of the successful defenders of T'an-ch'eng city in the fighting of 1641, had been unusually successful in continuing to collect taxes in the bleak days after the Manchu conquest of 1644, and he was publicly praised by the magistrate for his zeal. (He had two relatives who were also township heads, and perhaps the Yü family had particular expertise in this area, or special connections.) In 1671 he was still alive at the age of ninety, and Huang Liu-hung gave a banquet in his honor. But for many men the task was arduous, and it became common to appoint two men to share the post in a given township, with a yamen clerk assigned to assist the men in delivering the money collected.

The total population of T'an-ch'eng in 1670 was around 60,000; if there were about 15,000 people in each of the four districts, that would place some 1850 people in each township, scattered among a dozen or more villages. About one in six of these people was registered as an adult male (*ting*), aged between sixteen and sixty, and thus liable to corvée labor or payment of a commuted tax in lieu of that labor.

Since the rulers of the Ch'ing state were concerned with achieving thorough control over their subject population, this system of registration for taxation purposes was accompanied —at least on paper—by another system of registration and listing known as the *pao-chia* system. In many ways this overlapped with the taxation units, but the *pao-chia* had a more specifically police and militia function. Therefore the population of T'an-ch'eng county was registered in ascending circles—from the individual household, to the group of ten households, to ten groups of ten, and on to each district within the county. A modified version of the same system existed for the wards of the two main urban concentrations, T'an-ch'eng city and Ma-t'ou market, and for the more densely populated suburbs adjacent to them; a further modification existed for small or isolated village communities that numbered less than one hundred households. T'an-ch'eng city and Ma-t'ou market were the only large urban centers in the county at the time, though there were twenty-two areas designated as "markets" (*chi*); these overlapped with the thirty-two townships into which the county was divided.

Each commoner household was also expected to list its members in full, by sex, relationship, and age, servants and hired hands included—these were the so-called *pao-chia* registers, used for mutual security and responsibility in case of emergency for local crime. The names of the upper gentry, of senior and junior degree candidates, of Buddhist and Taoist monks and nuns had also to be reported in separate lists, although they were not included in the *pao-chia* tabulations. About two-fifths of the households were also expected to furnish a militiaman in emergencies, since they either had no member with any kind of literary degree, or no one serving in the yamen or the local government structure in any way, or were not exempt because the head-of-household was a widow or lacked descendants.

All these measures and regulations were allegedly in operation in T'an-ch'eng, but they had little effect on tax collection: by 1670 the county had been consistently in arrears for thirteen years.

On paper, at least, the basic tax rates in T'an-ch'eng were not excessive. The *ting* tax on registered individual males was 120 copper cash a year (0.12 taels*), assessed on 9498 persons, and yielding 1140 taels a year. (There were 242 members of the gentry and degree holders who were exempted from this payment.) The basic land tax was at a rate of 15.7 copper cash per *mou* (a *mou* being one-sixth of an acre); with 828,223 *mou* of registered land, that would bring in just over

---

* A tael was one ounce of silver and officially equivalent to one thousand copper cash.

13,000 taels a year. Basic expenses could be easily met from such revenues: a little over 7300 taels had to be sent to the Board of Revenue in Peking; 1125 went for the wages of the magistrate, his runners and porters, his doormen and chair carriers, the militia, and the police director and his staff. There were other minor expenses for ritual sacrifices, rewards to examination candidates, patrolmen for the county post-station inns, and prison maintenance, and at first sight it would seem that these could have been met by quite minor surcharges on the existing taxes, especially since the major costs of the regular military garrisons were met by provincial funds, and T'an-ch'eng had traditionally had low corvée quotas for river work.

The most important cause of the ongoing financial crisis in T'an-ch'eng stemmed from its geographical location on the eastern one of the two main roads to the south. This important strategic route led eventually to Chekiang and, beyond that, to the base of the southern feudatory Keng Ching-chung; it was a route both for military supplies and for communications—whether urgent or routine—sent along the government courier system. This meant that at any time people from T'an-ch'eng might be subjected to extraordinary demands for road maintenance or transport services, and in addition had the further expense of caring for officials and their retinues passing through. The situation was compounded by the relative poverty of this entire area of Shantung and by the shortage of horses and post stations. The T'an-ch'eng stations had to cover the forty miles of road north to I-chou, over thirty miles south to Ssu-wu, and not only the sixty miles westward to Yi-hsien, but another twenty-five miles beyond that, since Yi-hsien had no horses of its own. The government had assigned 3360 taels of T'an-ch'eng's tax monies to be used for the expenses of fodder, wages for grooms and couriers, equipment, and other stabling expenses; but this did not meet all the costs involved even for these items, nor did it cover veterinary costs and the purchase of extra horses. The result, as Feng K'o-ts'an wrote in the *Local History,* was that local officials in T'an-ch'eng were either forced into arrears with regular taxation deliveries or forced to neglect the horses under their care. (Feng knew what he was talking about, since he himself had lost his job for just such reasons.) Also, the temptations for local graft were massive, since fodder was costly, and the annual allowance for each horse in the two post stations was a little over thirty-two taels; obviously if one could draw the expenses for horses that were listed on the rolls but not actually in service, one could make a great deal of money, far more for example than by padding the rolls of the grooms, who earned 12.4 taels a year, or soldiers, who earned 6.

There had been a series of reforms, widespread in China since the late sixteenth century, which had led to many of the old corvée and service payments being commuted to silver; by 1670 the people of T'an-ch'eng paid most tax in silver, but several service taxes still remained: the collecting of great masses of willow branches, for example, to be bound up and used in shoring up the dikes on the Yellow River and Grand Canal; service in leading military horses to their destinations at various garrisons; escorting the mule trains carrying supplies; and furnishing special timber to the Board of Public Works for palace construction—this particular item had to be delivered all the way to Peking, a distance of over 550 miles. Furthermore, though there had not customarily been a demand on T'an-ch'eng workers for service on the Yellow River and Grand Canal, because of the poverty of the county and its distance from the main waterways, this policy had been reversed in the early 1650s, again in 1666, and yet again in 1670 for the vast dredging and diking project on Lake E-ma to the south. Huang Liu-hung wrote of the people of T'an-ch'eng being sent nearly one hundred miles, without proper food or shelter, to work on this million-tael project. "Once they had died or fled," he wrote, "how would they ever be put to work again? And how would the ravaged lands in their own county ever be opened up again for cultivation?"

Certainly in the years prior to the earthquake the government had responded generously enough by reducing basic quotas to correspond with the levels of disaster in the county. Thus in the late Ming, T'an-ch'eng had a quota of 40,002 able-bodied males eligible for corvée; this figure dropped by 3540 in the famine of 1640, because of death or flight; it dropped by another 2734 men in 1641, killed when bandits destroyed Ma-t'ou and other nearby market towns; and dropped again by 790 later in the year, that being the number who died in the epidemics following the raids. That would have made the total of corvée males in the county 32,938 when the Manchus attacked in 1643. The *Local History* records that the slaughter was so terrible that "only three or four were left alive out of every ten"; if we take this statement literally as a 30 per cent survival rate, we would be left with a figure of 9881 corvée males, which accords well with the new quota given for the county by the government in 1646 of 9927. This number, after some initial resettlement in the area, was lowered even further to the 1670 figure of 9498, because of the earthquake of 1668 (though, as we have seen, the local officials did not find this an adequate response). Similarly, the number of officially listed townships shrank from eighty-five to thirty-two, and the area of land assessed for tax purposes was lowered over the same period by almost one-third.

This drop in registered land suggests one of two things: either labor was in such short supply that a large percentage of the land in T'an-ch'eng was abandoned, or the chaos of the times was so intense that landlords were able to remove their land from the tax registers and make sure that it stayed off. If the second alternative is the right one, then it was more likely that larger landowners rather than small peasant proprietors had the influence to achieve the desired result—and the tax boon to them may have been even larger than it looks, since the registered "fiscal acre" might in fact be composed of two or three acres of poor land that could be expected to produce the same amount of crops as one fertile acre. The *Local History* asserts that when land in T'an-ch'eng was given the lowest rating on the nine-point scale, then it was truly terrible land—prone to flooding from the I and Shu rivers or their tributaries, staying water-logged through the summer: to expect a harvest regularly from such land was like "looking for yields from a field of rocks," and at the best one could "hope for one good harvest out of every ten." But the *Local History* remarks neither on how many people sought to register land in such a category, nor on whether a landlord family with the resources to drain such land effectively was ever reclassified back into a higher tax assessment.

Sometimes the various categories of hardship overlapped, as in the area of Feng-shan township on the I River, which bordered on the jurisdictions of T'an-ch'eng and I-chou. The tax problems here had grown so complex that Huang Liu-hung and the I-chou magistrate were ordered out in the middle of winter to investigate what was happening. Riding through the township in the snow and interviewing the locals, they found twelve small villages, scattered over half a dozen miles, that had received differing degrees of flood damage over the last two decades and were in a desperate situation; about half of the three hundred households that once farmed there had fled or died. Large landholdings had been abandoned by their landlords, so the land was no longer registered in any-one's name for tax purposes. Around 1600 acres registered as "sandy soil" had once produced crops even during moderate floods; and for twenty-five years, the farmers pointed out, they had paid some taxes, because at least things had been better than during the years 1640–1643. But the massive flooding after the 1668 earthquake had washed more sand onto the fields, so the farmers could no longer pay anything at all. In such cases it took prolonged appeals by the local farmers—in conjunction with an appeal by the magistrate to the prefect—before the land was formally removed from the tax rolls.

Even if the local farmers had the surplus grain or money to pay taxes with, their problems were not necessarily over. There was the problem of assayers, who had the monopoly of converting the farmers' copper cash into the silver that was required for tax payment: some assayers cheated on the purity of the metal, some concealed fragments of the metal while shaping the ingots, some charged large extra fees for applying the seals that stated the purity of the metal, some charged extra to work a little faster—knowing full well that if they worked slowly the farmers would have the extra expense of an overnight stay in the city—and some indulged in such extreme forms of cheating as kicking over the melting pot before the silver had been properly weighed out. On other occasions, if the country people brought their grain to the city in person, they were met by "helpful" townsfolk who offered to conduct their business for them while they rested, took the grain (allegedly to the taxation depot), and then never returned with the money. For these and other reasons, said Huang Liu-hung, countrymen looked upon "the city as hell, the clerks as ghosts." Part of the object of the decentralization under the thirty-two township heads was to have local taxation pickup points so that the farmers would not have to go into T'an-ch'eng city at all. Instead, large tax-collection chests were installed at more convenient points, and the money paid into these chests was (at least theoretically) carefully checked on a daily roster, with correct receipts issued in triplicate: one copy for the payee, one for the collector, and one for the magistrate's files.

Taxes on land and agricultural production were not the

only ones levied in T'an-ch'eng. There were taxes in the forms of objects or produce that had to be sent to Peking, and concealed taxes in the form of produce bought from the locals by the government at far below its cost price. There were taxes on the reed beds, which could be gathered for roofing and fuel, taxes on fishermen, taxes on street peddlers, and taxes (prepaid by the merchants) on every ounce of salt that was sold. There were taxes on every transaction that the licensed brokers performed in real-estate or land sales. There were taxes of five taels a year on every licensed pawnshop— though exemptions were given for deals in which desperate peasants were pawning their farm tools for grain. There were sales taxes on all brokers' dealings in livestock and tobacco, cotton goods, wines, and grain for making fermented liquor. There was a "meltage fee" for converting taxes paid in copper to silver of the accepted standard.

The collection of these extra taxes could be a nightmare for payer and collector alike, as P'u Sung-ling pointed out in the opening lines of his sardonic story "The Fighting Cricket":

"The Court took much delight in playing with fighting crickets, and ordered an annual quota of them from the people. These insects used not to be reared in the western part of the country until the magistrate of Hua-yin, eager to make up to his superior, gave him a present of one that was a skilled fighter; thenceforth his superior demanded a regular supply, and the magistrate passed this order down to the village headmen. The result was that ne'er-do-wells in the town sought for fine crickets and raised them carefully; the price of the insects went up and up, and they were treated as objects of rarity. The headmen's own tough subordinates used this fact when they went to collect the tax levies, and the furnishing of a single cricket could ruin the resources of several households.

"Out in the countryside lived a man named Ch'eng who kept failing at the lower examinations; since he was rather stupid, the local toughs recommended him for the position of headman. Ch'eng did everything he could to get out of it, but could not avoid the job. Before a year was out his resources were all gone; when the time came to supply the quota of crickets, Ch'eng, who did not dare put pressure on his neighbors yet could not raise the sum himself, wished in his grief to put an end to his life. . . ."

Pressures, levies, and deadlines were commonplace in T'an-ch'eng, as Huang Liu-hung knew. He would have liked to reduce some of the pressures on the country people by increasing taxation on the townsmen, since he was convinced that the taxes on urban commercial transactions could be made to yield far more than they did; he guessed that not more than 20 per cent of taxable commercial transactions were ever reported, and even from Ma-t'ou market he only collected a little under 500 taels: 230 from the sheds of the salt picklers that ran along the I River, and some 250 from the brokers handling long-distance shipments of cloth and foodstuffs, wine and tobacco. Yet Huang was unable to remedy this state of affairs. One trouble was that the urban population was not easy to control; it was prone to riot over economic grievances, and the more wealthy merchants were not T'an-ch'eng men at all: the majority were from Shansi in the northwest, though there were also many from Kiangsu to the south. They were thus able to exert pressures on those local officials who hailed from their native provinces. The two market headmen of Ma-t'ou at this time were both involved in law cases that showed their weakness and vulnerability: Ch'eng Yü had been framed in a complicated corruption charge by the manager of the local distilled-liquor guild; Chang Mao-te had had his grain supply stolen by two soldiers. When Chang complained to their superiors, the soldiers returned with reinforcements and savagely beat him; "the wounds covered his body as the scales cover the fish," reported the police official who examined the victim shortly afterward.

Several barriers to fair and adequate tax collection were erected by the soldiers in T'an-ch'eng, for they caused trouble out of all proportion to their numbers. They not only feuded with the grooms and postal-system staff, but they were also violent with members of the magistrate's own staff: the squad leader Chang San let his wife sickle the grain in people's fields, and later turned some of his squad against the police constable who came to press him for tax payments. Another soldier stood by while his son bloodied the face of one of the yamen runners with a cudgel. A third entered the house of constable Chao, helped himself to drink, and raped Chao's wife. Other soldiers, like Sang Ssu from the garrison in I-chou, had managed to accumulate land holdings of over four hundred *mou,* on which he paid no taxes whatsoever; he also beat up the runner who tried to collect tax from him. On other occasions the details of land ownership were so tangled that it was virtually impossible to sort out to whom a given piece of property belonged, with overlapping claims going back into the Ming dynasty, with contracts issued and voided in the 1650s, and with litigants reckless enough to insert forged versions of findings in their favor, dated many years previously, into the magistrate's own back files in the yamen.

In T'an-ch'eng, Huang Liu-hung had found, the landlords used six major types of deception to lower their land tax assessments. They hired managers to run their land under assumed names so that they could not be tracked down and held accountable. They pretended that their land was in fact owned by families living in another jurisdiction. They would hand in their taxes in cash or grain as part of a neighboring family's own tax quota—when that neighboring family was paying at a lower rate. They managed falsely to declare the quality of their land, registering (for example) middle-grade land assessed at 30 per cent as being lowest grade (20 per cent) or the highest (50 per cent) as being middle. They kept their land out of the registers altogether. They declared that the grain they had grown on their own land had been produced on someone else's land. In T'an-ch'eng these problems were exacerbated by the fact that a good deal of local land had been bought at cheap prices by landlords who lived in I-chou, hence out of the local magistrate's jurisdiction.

This kind of graft was carried out by landlords entirely in their own interest: as Huang Liu-hung put it, "They want to make a large grain production look small so that they can get out of a heavy tax levy." Even more complex was the system by which certain landlords took over the tax responsibilities of others in the system of protection and proxy remittances known as *pao-lan*. This system was particularly used by those who wanted to avoid the service levies owed by each registered adult; since landlords with examination degrees were exempt from much of the service tax, their poor relations and friends, or other wealthy neighbors, would make their land over to such privileged families, so that they themselves paid tax at a lower rate, as well as shared in certain other privileges such as paying the lower "meltage fees" or using the tax-receipt boxes in the county city, where the gentry could get certain auxiliary charges waived. The poor actively sought to get in on such proxy relationships, both for the tax advantages and for the protection against the magistrate's staff that the rich household could give them. In return the landlords got prestige and loyal followers. Upper gentry might have several dozen such semidependents, known as "bonded adults," and even low-level degree candidates had ten or more. As a result, the local headmen responsible for apportioning service tasks, or registering new able-bodied males in the county lists, would keep away from the "bonded adults" and pile even heavier assessments on those who were without such backing; the result was that an annual levy, which should have been around one-tenth of a tael, rose for many of the poor to be one or even two taels in a given year, a sum that they could not possibly afford.

In the late spring of 1671 locusts hatched out in the fields from eggs that had been laid there the previous year. In a specially composed prayer to the God of T'an-ch'eng City—the most important of the local gods, and the one directly responsible for the welfare of its people—Huang tried to sway the god with a combination of reason and emotion, in order to prevent another crisis being added to all the others. His prayer was given added urgency by local memories of the terrible locust plague and famine of 1640:

O City God, both of us have duties to perform in this county: resisting disasters that may occur, offering protection in times of trouble, such things are in the City God's spiritual realm and are part of the official's responsibilities. This year, while the workers were out in the fields but the grain had not yet matured, the eggs that had been laid by last year's locusts hatched out in the soil, causing almost half the wheat crops in the countryside to suffer this affliction. In the last ten days yet more locusts have come from our neighboring area to the southwest*: their trembling wings stretch in unbroken lines, they fill in the furrows and cover the ridges of the fields. The people scurry and wail, as if the end of the world were come.

We have already prayed to the City God, but he did not destroy the locusts. Could this possibly have been because it was too hard for him to save us from this natural calamity? Or because the Ch'ing-ming festival† was near at hand? If not for those reasons, then was it because the officials had failed in their duties, and lacked the sincerity to reach the underworld? The people could not repel this calamity, so they appealed to the officials for help. The officials could not repel this calamity for the people, so they pray to the City God. The City God is majestic on high; could He not transmit these prayers from the people and from their officials, and petition the Lord of All? The people think

---

* I.e., from the county of P'ei.
† Fourth month, fifth day of the lunar calendar.

that the spread of this disaster is unavoidable, for as the locusts advance they cover an area of over a thousand *li*, in the midst of which T'an-ch'eng is but a tiny spot, so how could they be chased away just from here? They say this because they have no remedy if they use human means. But that is not true of the City God. From his vantage point he can anticipate the needs of the people and officials, and feel sorrow for their sufferings.

O God, drive them away quickly! Do not let them destroy our crops of grain! Do not let them lay their eggs in our fields! Then will the people have an autumn harvest. God grant this. God heed our request.

P'u Sung-ling did not believe that local officials could handle these problems of tax collection and natural disasters any better than they could control local banditry; if anything, his skepticism here was even greater. And so we find that his remarkable protagonist Hsiao-erh, who more than any of P'u's other characters is able to save a community from economic collapse, is also nearer than most of his other characters to direct sources of heavenly aid:

Chao Wang and his wife, who lived in the country of T'eng, were devout Buddhists. They ate no meat or forbidden foods, and in their district they were regarded as worthy people. They were quite prosperous and had a daughter, Hsiao-erh, who was unusually intelligent and beautiful. Chao loved her like a jewel.

At the age of five she was sent off to study with a teacher, as was her elder brother Ch'ang-ch'un; after five years she had mastered the Five Classics. In her class was a boy named Ting Tzu-mo, three years her senior and stylishly cultured; the two fell in love and Ting privately let his mother know his feelings. She in turn asked the Chaos if her son might marry their daughter, but since they had hopes that she would marry into a wealthy family, they refused to allow the engagement.

Shortly after this, Chao was converted by the White Lotus sect; and when Hsü Hung-ju rebelled, the whole family were implicated as rebels. Hsiao-erh, being well educated and quick-witted, was able to grasp at one glance the magical skills with which one transformed paper into soldiers or beans into horses: she was much the best of the six young girls whom Hsü selected for special training, and so he initiated her into all his techniques. Because of her achievements her father, Chao, was also given important assignments.

When Ting was seventeen he passed the licentiate's examinations in T'eng, but was unwilling to discuss marriage with any-one, since he could never get Hsiao-erh out of his mind; so he slipped away and enrolled under Hsü's standard. Hsiao-erh was delighted to see him and showed him favors far beyond the ordinary. Since she was Hsü's disciple, and Hsü had put her in charge of military affairs, she was fully occupied, being in and out of his office day and night, and she had not even a moment to spare for her parents. Yet whenever Ting came to see her in the evenings, she sent the servants away, and they would stay together until the small hours. One night he asked her secretly, "Do you know the real reason why I came here to you?" She replied that she didn't. "I have no crazy dreams of honor," said Ting; "the reason I came here was because of you. This evil Way will not succeed; it is bound to end in disaster. You are an intelligent woman, can't you see that? If you run away from here with me you will find you can trust my loyalty completely."

Hsiao-erh seemed sorrowful for a while; then, as if wakening from a dream, she said, "It would not be proper to just turn my back on my parents and leave. Please let me tell them."

So the two of them went to tell her parents of their hopes and fears, but Chao could not grasp what they were saying. "My teacher is a god," he said. "How could he make any errors?" Hsiao-erh knew she could admonish them no further, and changed her hair style from the tufts of the child to the chignon of the married woman.

She took two paper kites; she straddled one and Ting the other. Majestically the kites spread out their wings like two great Chien birds; they spread their wings and off they flew. At dawn they reached the borders of Lai-wu county. The girl squeezed the neck of her kite, and immediately the two kites landed gently on the ground and changed into two donkeys, on which the couple galloped off to the village of Shan-yin-li. There they claimed to be refugees from the current turmoils, rented a house, and settled in. The two of them had left in a great hurry; they had almost no possessions and nothing to buy any with. Ting took this much to heart and tried to borrow a little rice from the neighbors, but none of them was willing to let him have even the smallest amount. Hsiao-erh didn't seem at all depressed, however, but went and pawned her hairpins and earrings.

Closing their door, she would seat herself tranquilly opposite Ting, and they would play together at guessing games in the lamplight, or see who could remember most from the books they had read in order to see which of them was the superior; the loser would have to bend his fingers painfully down onto his wrist.

West of their house lived a neighbor called Weng, a leading figure among the local outlaws, and one day when he came back from a raid, Hsiao-erh said to Ting, "With such a wealthy neighbor, what should we be worrying about? Let's see if he will make us a short-term loan of one thousand taels." Ting thought that that would be very difficult, but she replied, "I'll fix things so that he'll be delighted to help us." So saying, she cut a sheet of paper into the silhouette of the Judge of the Underworld, put the silhouette on the ground, and placed a chicken cage over it. Taking Ting by the hand, she climbed onto the bed, heated up some fine old wine, and used the *Rituals of the Chou Dynasty* as the source for a new game: each would name such-and-such a volume, such-and-such a page, such-and-such a line of the text; if, upon checking the point chosen, there was an ideogram with the radical for food, water, or liquor, then the chooser drank a forfeit; if the phrase contained the wine radical, then the loser drank double. Hsiao-erh happened to hit upon the word "wine," and Ting made her drink a mug of wine; in return she vowed, "If we are to receive the money you must hit on an ideogram for 'drinking.'" Ting made his choice in the book and came up with "turtle." Hsiao-erh roared with laughter—"We've as good as made it"—and filled a wine cup drop by drop for Ting to drink; as he protested, she pointed out, "Your job involves water, so you must drink as the turtle does." They were still arguing over the decision when they heard a tap-tapping in the cage, and Hsiao-erh got up and called out, "It's here." Lifting the cage, she looked inside, and there was a bag full of lumps of gold. Ting couldn't hide his surprise and joy.

A little time later one of Weng's maidservants, carrying a baby, came over to relax with them for a bit, and told them this: "When my master came home he lit the lamp and sat down for the evening; suddenly an unfathomable crevasse opened in the earth, and one of the Judges of the Underworld emerged and said to him, 'I am an official from Below, and the Master of T'ai-shan gathered us all together to make a record of the evil deeds of all criminals; I must provide one thousand silver lamps, each of which weighs ten ounces; if you donate one hundred lamps I will exonerate you from your crimes.' My master was terrified, burned incense and prostrated himself in prayer, and made an offering of one thousand taels. At which the Judge of the Underworld softly faded back into the earth, which closed up after him." Both the man and the woman, on hearing these words, clucked away in feigned astonishment.

After this the couple started to buy cattle and horses, hired servants and maids, and built themselves a dwelling. But their wealth attracted the attention of a local ne'er-do-well; he assembled a group of ruffians and broke into their home to pillage. Ting and his wife were awakened from their dreams; lighting a torch of grasses, they saw that their house was filled with thieves. Two of the thieves seized Ting, while a third ran his hands over Hsiao-erh's breasts. She sat up, stark naked, pointed her finger at them, and cried out, "Halt! Halt!" The thirteen thieves, tongues protruding, stood motionless, idiots, as if made of wood. Hsiao-erh dressed and climbed down from the bed, called her servants to her, and had them tie the thieves' arms behind their backs, one by one, while she made them confess to their plot; she reproached them, saying, "We came from far away to hide ourselves among your hills, trusting that we would get help from you; how could you have acted with so little humanity? All of us have periods of ease and periods of crisis; those who are in bad trouble had only to tell us; we are not the kind of people to hoard everything up for ourselves. You have acted like wolves and deserve to die, but since I am sorry for you, I shall let you go—though I will not forgive you if you do wrong again!" The thieves all prostrated themselves in thanks and went away.

Some time later the White Lotus leader, Hsü Hung-ju, was captured, and Hsiao-erh's parents, Mr. and Mrs. Chao, together with their son and daughter-in-law, were all executed. Ting went off with some money and ransomed the little three-year-old son of Hsiao-erh's dead brother, Ch'ang-ch'un; they brought him up as their own son and gave him the surname Ting and the personal name of Ch'eng-t'iao [son with two ancestral halls], so the villagers gradually came to realize that the couple were related to members of the White Lotus sect. At this time there happened to be locusts destroying the crops, and Hsiao-erh made hundreds of kites out of paper and sent them to patrol her fields, so that the locusts all flew elsewhere and left her fields alone, undamaged; accordingly, the other villagers were all jealous and denounced the couple to the local officials as being survivors of Hsü Hung-ju's sect. The local mandarin also had his eye on their wealth, and saw them as a fat prize, so he arrested Ting; Ting bought back his freedom by paying a massive bribe, but Hsiao-erh said, "We obtained our wealth by improper means, it will inevitably melt away; nevertheless we can live no longer in this district of snakes and scorpions." So they sold off all their holdings, cheaply, and left.

They moved to the western suburbs of the district capital. Now Hsiao-erh was extraordinarily clever; she was good at handling money and better than any man at running a business. She opened up a factory for making objects out of glass, and herself instructed all the workers who came to work there; the result was that all the lamps made there had the most curious forms and magical colors, none of her competitors could match them, and she sold them without any trouble at high prices. After a few years they were richer than ever.

Hsiao-erh watched strictly over her servants and maids, and of the hundreds she fed every one had some function. When she had leisure time she and Ting brewed tea and played a game of chess, or they played their games of scanning through the Classics and the Histories. Every five days she went through the accounts, checking on the inflow and outflow of money and grain and on the tasks performed by the servants: as Ting checked off their names on the lists, and the amount of work they had done, Hsiao-erh assigned them each different tallies; those who had been diligent received various rewards, while the lazy were whipped and made to stay kneeling for a long stretch of time. On some days she granted a holiday and demanded no work in the evening; she and her husband laid out food and wine and then invited the servants to come and sing their local folk songs so that all could enjoy themselves.

Hsiao-erh's acuity was like a god's, and no one dared to try and deceive her; besides which she gave higher recompense for work done than was really justified, so everything went smoothly. There were more than two hundred families in her village, and to all the poor she gave a certain amount of working capital, with the result that there were no drifters or unemployed in her district. When droughts came she had the villagers build an altar out in the countryside and had herself carried there at night; after she performed the rites of "The Steps of Emperor Yü," refreshing rains fell, and there was enough for everyone in an area five *li* around. So people thought her even more like a god.

When she went out on excursions she made no attempt to cover her face, and all the people in her village saw her; sometimes the young men of the village would gather together and talk about her beauty privately to each other, but when she appeared in person before them they hushed their chatter and dared not even raise their eyes to look at her.

Every autumn she gave some money to the village children who were not yet big enough to work in the fields, and sent them off to collect wild sow thistles; after twenty years of this she had filled buildings with the plants. People thought this was silly and mocked her in private; but when there was a great famine in Shantung, and people began to eat each other, Hsiao-erh took out these leaves she had saved, mixed them with grain, and gave them to the starving. So it was that the nearby villagers were able to stay alive. They did not have to run away or die.

P'u Sung-ling must have got the idea of using this glass-lantern factory as a resource for the whole community from the real glass factory that was operating at this time in Po-shan county, just south of his home town of Tzu-ch'uan. But there was no such local industry in T'an-ch'eng, and Huang Liu-hung had neither outside sources of income to draw on nor any magical formulas for separating the T'an-ch'eng gentry—whether criminal or respectable—from their money. He knew from experience that gentry could not be treated like commoners when it came to tax collection: commoners would usually pay out of fear, if pressed hard enough, but with gentry there was always delay and the danger of making them lose face if one pushed them too hard; this could lead to local antagonisms and even to appeals over the magistrate's head to other officials, or else to harassment of his staff.

Yet Huang finally decided he had to take action against one particular landlord, Liu T'ing-yüan, of Hsin-wang township, seven miles west of T'an-ch'eng city and near Ma-t'ou. Hsin-wang was one of four townships in the county that were particularly notorious for proxy corruption, the others being Chu-lu and Chung-kou in the northeast of the county, and Hsing-shu to the south. Most of these townships were also notorious for the length of time they had been in arrears, and Huang Liu-hung had tried to raise the morale of the taxpayers by promising ritual wine, garlands, ceremonial clothes, and a send-off through the main gate of the yamen to all those who paid up on time. This had not helped in Hsin-wang, where over half the people were in a proxy relationship to some landlord or other, and those who had not been able to find such protection were fleeing in increasing numbers, making the payments even higher for those who remained.

In 1671 the two township heads in Hsin-wang were Hu Chi-ming and a colleague also named Hu; by the late spring they were desperate at their inability to extract taxation from the community caught in its circle of evasion, proxy relationships, and flight. In their desperation they agreed to give testimony against the landlord Liu T'ing-yüan, who, though he held his land in Hsin-wang, had made his personal residence in the township of Kao-ts'e, just next to the county city. The Lius were one of the two lineages that dominated Kao-ts'e, and they could provide a safe haven there for any fugitives. Though the two Hus decided to give testimony against Liu in the magistrate's court, they asked to be given an extension until all the winter-wheat crops had been harvested, in the hopes that they could raise enough money from the farmers (once more sales had been made) to meet the first part of their quotas.

The landlord Liu T'ing-yüan acted swiftly to take advantage of this pause. He stationed a hired thug outside the magistrate's court to intimidate witnesses who might come to give evidence against the Liu family, and with another group of henchmen he tracked down the two Hus, beat them savagely, and broke their legs. Not content with that, he had Hu Chiming's battered body slung from a pole and carried out of T'an-ch'eng altogether, into I-chou, so as to delay the whole investigation further. Liu himself then fled from T'an-ch'eng and hid out elsewhere. No other witnesses could be found who were willing to testify, so the case was suspended.

❋

Three

THE
WIDOW

❋

WOMAN P'ENG'S HUSBAND, Ch'en T'ai-chen, died of illness in 1669. He had not been wealthy, but he left her a little money, some land near T'an-ch'eng city, a house, and an ox. They had one child, a boy called Lien, and it now became the widow's responsibility to raise and educate him so that he might worthily carry on his father's line.

The *Local History* contains numerous biographies designed to show how—with determination and strict moral purpose— one could survive as a widow, make a living, and bring up one's children to be either worthy scholars or loyal wives in their turn. One woman was widowed at twenty-one and left with three sons; she brought them all up successfully, and lived to be eighty-four. Woman Li, widowed with two sons, sent one off to work the land and put aside money from her spinning to educate the other; he passed the local examina- tions and went on to pass the provincial level *chü-jen* ex- amination (one of the five from T'an-ch'eng in a century to attain that honor). Both these women were dead by 1670, but many others were alive to bear testimony to the ideal: Woman Tu, whose husband and his brothers were all killed by the Manchus in 1643, had brought up her own two sons as well as three orphaned nephews and two nieces; she was fifty-five. Woman Liu, widowed and childless at twenty-five, had adopted a son from her husband's uncle to continue her husband's blood line and be his legal heir; she was forty-six. Woman T'ien was fifty-six, having been widowed when pregnant at the age of nineteen, and brought her son up to manhood. The paragon of them all was woman Fan, of Leng-ts'un township, still living at eighty-one, having brought up her own son, her husband's first wife's two sons, and her own orphaned grandson, all to be successful candidates in the local examinations.

P'u Sung-ling had an ambiguous attitude toward such accounts, and he could at times mock the alleged probity of these widows so busy with their spinning:

An old widow was spinning one evening when suddenly a young girl pushed open the door and said with a laugh, "Old woman, aren't you tired?" The girl looked eighteen or nineteen; her face was beautiful, her clothes were bright and elegant. Startled, the old woman asked her where she came from, and the girl replied, "I pitied your lonely life and came to keep you company." The old woman suspected that she had run away from some wealthy home, and kept on questioning her insistently. But the girl said, "Old woman, don't be afraid. I am alone in the world, just as you are. Admiring the purity of your life, I came to be with you; if we stay together, we can avoid loneliness—isn't that the best thing?" The old woman suspected that she must be a fox spirit, and stayed silent and suspicious. The girl climbed up onto the frame and started spinning in her place, saying, "You don't have to worry. I'm good at making my own living in this way, and you won't have to support me." When the old lady saw how friendly and helpful she was, and how sweet, she felt at ease.

When it grew quite dark, the girl said to the old woman, "I brought with me my covers and pillow, and they are still outside the door. When you go out to relieve yourself, please bring them in for me." The old woman went out and found a bag of clothes, and the girl laid them out on the bed; they were of some kind of brocaded fabric, incomparably fragrant and soft; the old woman laid out her own cotton quilt and lay down on the bed with the girl. Hardly had the girl slipped off her silken dress than a strange scent filled the room; and as they lay there the old woman thought to herself, What a shame to be next to such a beauty and not to have a man's body. From her pillow the girl smiled and said, "You're an old woman of seventy, how can you still have such reckless thoughts?" And the old woman replied, "I wasn't." The girl said, "If you are not having reckless thoughts, why were you wishing that you were a man?" The old woman was now all the more sure she was dealing with a fox spirit, and grew frightened. At which the girl smiled again, saying, "You are the one who wants to be a man, how can it be that you are afraid of me?"

P'u Sung-ling also mocked the gentry—the self-same men who compiled the biographies of the honorable and virtuous —for their combination of fastidiousness and lechery, the very characteristics that they lavishly praised others for not having. And he implied that they often had ambiguous motives for including women in their lists of the "virtuous." P'u's suspicions are borne out well enough by examples from T'an-ch'eng, at least at one level, since Feng K'o-ts'an mentions that he drew the material for the biographies in the "honorable and virtuous" sections of his *Local History* from the local gentry. There is no doubt that these sections reflect gentry values or an idealized version of them; we can also tell that the gentry practiced a form of historiographical nepotism, since four of the local compilers managed between them to include three of their mothers and two sisters-in-law among the chosen fifty-six.

But in general P'u seems to have subscribed to the prevailing views concerning the need for widows' morality and fixity of purpose. Thus in one of his stories a widow is expressly given permission to remarry by her dying husband, but when she violates propriety by taking a lover before the funeral ceremonies are completed, the dead husband wreaks divine vengeance on her and her family: her naked body, transfixed with arrows, is found lying in the garden of her father's burning house. P'u differs, however, from most of his contemporaries in that he often describes his fictional widows as being knowledgeable about the law and familiar with the intricacies of yamen politics, quite able to outwit the men who try to rob them of their lands or their good names. He was always particularly intrigued by the problems that a widow faced as she tried to bring up a family of boys; and in one of his sterner stories, "Hsi-liu," he amplifies the predicament by having as heroine a woman who not only had not wanted to marry her husband in the first place but had been left a stepson to bring up alongside her own son:

H si-liu was the daughter of a scholar living in Chung-tu. She was given this name—which means "delicate willow" —because her waist was so incomparably slender.

She was an intelligent girl with a good grasp of literature and had a particular fondness for books on human physiognomy. Easygoing by nature, she was not one to criticize others; but whenever anyone came to make inquiries about possibly marrying her, she always insisted on taking a personal look at the suitor, and though she examined many men, she found them all wanting. By the time she was nineteen her parents had grown angry, and said to her, "How can there be no mate suitable for you on this earth? Do you want to keep your girlish braids until you're an old woman?"

Hsi-liu replied, "I had truly hoped that with my human forces

I could overcome the divine forces, but I have not succeeded over these many years and can see that it is my fate. From this time on I will ask no more than to obey my parents' commands."

At this time it happened that there was a scholar named Kao, from a good family and known for his abilities, who asked for Hsi-liu's hand in marriage and sent over the bridal gifts. So the ceremonies were performed.

Husband and wife got on well together. Kao had a son of five from a former marriage, named Ch'ang-fu, and Hsi-liu looked after the boy so lovingly that if she had to go off and visit her parents, he yelled and wept and tried to follow her, and no amount of scolding would make him stop. After a little over a year Hsi-liu gave birth to a son of her own, and named him Ch'ang-hu —"the reliable one." When her husband asked what the name signified, she answered, "Only that I hope he will remain long with his parents."

Hsi-liu was cursory over woman's work and seemed to take little interest in it; but she pored carefully over the records in which the acreage of their properties and the size of their tax assessment were listed, and worried if anything was not exactly accurate. After a time she said to Kao, "Would you be willing to give up attending to our family's business affairs and let me look after them?" Kao let her take over; for six months everything went well with the family's affairs, and Kao praised her.

One day Kao went off to a neighboring village to drink wine with friends, and while he was away one of the local tax collectors came, demanding payment. He banged on the door and cursed at Hsi-liu; she sent one of her maids to calm him down, but since he wouldn't go away, she had to send one of the menservants to go and fetch her husband home. When Kao returned, the man left. Kao laughed and said, "Hsi-liu, do you now begin to see why an intelligent woman can never be the match for a stupid man?"

When Hsi-liu heard these words she lowered her head and

began to cry; worried, Kao drew her to him and tried to encourage her, but for a long time she could not be comforted. He was unhappy that she was so caught up in running the household affairs, and suggested that he take them over again himself, but she wouldn't let him.

She rose at dawn, and retired late, and managed everything with the greatest diligence. She would put aside the money for each year's taxes a year in advance, and no more did the runners sent to press for payments come to her door; in the same way she calculated in advance for their food and clothing needs, and thus their expenditure was controlled. Kao was delighted, and playfully said to her, "How can my 'delicate willow' be so delicate? Your eyebrows are delicate, your waist is delicate, your little feet are delicate; but I am delighted that your determination is even more delicate than those."

And Hsi-liu replied, "My husband's name means 'high,' and you are truly high: your character is high, your ambitions are high, your scholarship is high; but what I hope is that the number of your years will be even higher."

There was, in their village, a dealer who sold beautiful coffins, and Hsi-liu insisted on buying one regardless of the cost; since she didn't have enough money, she raised it by asking around among her relatives and neighbors. Kao did not see the urgency for the purchase and tried to stop her, but she paid him no heed. About a year later there was a death in a wealthy neighboring family, and they offered her double what the coffin had cost; the profit would have been so good that Kao urged his wife to accept the offer, but she wouldn't do it. He asked why not. She did not reply. He asked her again, and her eyes glistened with tears. Kao was surprised but did not want to contradict her directly, so he left the matter there.

Another year went by, and Kao was now twenty-five. Hsi-liu would not let him go away on long journeys, and if he was late coming back from some visit, she would send the servants over to ask him to return, and they would follow him back down the roads. Kao's friends all joked with him about this.

One day Kao was out drinking with some friends; he felt there was something wrong with him and started for home, but halfway back he fell from his horse and died. The weather at this time was damp and hot, but fortunately all his burial clothes had been made ready in advance. The villagers all praised Hsi-liu for her foresight.

Her stepson, Ch'ang-fu, was now ten years old and just beginning to learn essay writing, but after his father died he grew peevish and lazy and refused to study. He would run off and follow the herdsboys on their outings—scolding him had no effect, and even after beatings he continued his wanton behavior. Hsi-liu had no remedy left, so she called him to her and said, "You have shown that you don't want to study; how is there any way that we can force you? But in poor households there can be none without employment, so change your clothes and go and work alongside the servants. If you don't, I'll have you beaten, and it will be too late for regrets." So in ripped, wadded clothes Ch'ang-fu went to herd the pigs, and when he came home after work he took his pottery bowl and joined the other servants for a meal of gruel. After a few days he had suffered enough and, weeping, knelt outside the family courtyard, begging to be allowed to study again. Hsi-liu turned away from him toward the wall as if she hadn't even heard him, and there was nothing for Ch'ang-fu to do but pick up his whip, swallow his tears, and depart. As autumn came to an end Ch'ang-fu had no clothes for his body and no shoes for his feet; the freezing rain soaked into his body and he carried his head hunched into his shoulders like a beggar. The villagers all pitied him, and those who had children from a former marriage took Hsi-liu as a warning. They murmured angrily against her, and Hsi-liu gradually became aware of it, but ignored them as if it were nothing to do with her. Finally Ch'ang-fu could bear the hardship no more; he abandoned his pigs and ran away. Still Hsi-liu took no action, neither sending anyone to check on him nor even making inquiries about him. After a few more months there was nowhere left for Ch'ang-fu to beg for food, and deeply grieving, he returned home. Yet he dared not enter, and begged an old woman neighbor to go and tell his mother he was back. Hsi-liu said, "If he will accept a beating of one hundred blows he can come in and see me; if not, then let him be on his way again."

Ch'ang-fu heard this and ran in, weeping that he would gladly receive the blows. "Do you now understand how to change your ways and repent?" she asked.

"I repent," he said.

And his mother responded, "If you know how to repent, then there is no need to give you a beating. Go in peace and tend to your pigs; if you behave badly again, there will be no forgiveness."

Ch'ang-fu cried out, "I'd be happy to receive the hundred blows if you would let me study again."

Hsi-liu made no response, but when the old woman added her own pleas, she finally agreed. She gave him a bath and some clothes and sent him off to study with the same teacher as his younger brother. Ch'ang-fu worked diligently and well, far differently from the past, and after three years he passed the local district examinations. Governor Yang saw his essays and was impressed; he had Ch'ang-fu given a monthly stipend to help him along with the cost of his studies.

Ch'ang-hu, on the other hand, was incredibly stupid; after studying for several years he still could not remember the ideographs for his own name. Hsi-liu told him to put away his books and go out and work in the fields, but he preferred to fool around and showed himself unwilling to take the pains of hard work. His mother said angrily, "Each of the four classes has its occupation, but since you are incapable of study and unable to work in the fields, how are you going to avoid dying in some ditch?" She had him beaten, and from then on he went out with the hired hands to work in the fields. If he was late getting up, then she scolded him and followed after him, cursing. And secretly she began to give the best there was in clothing, food, and drink to his elder brother, Ch'ang-fu. Although Ch'ang-hu dared not complain, he could not avoid being deeply upset.

When the year's work in the fields was over, Hsi-liu took some money and gave it to Ch'ang-hu so that he could learn the ways of a traveling peddler; but Ch'ang-hu, who had a passion for gambling, lost all the money she gave him and then, in an attempt to deceive her, made up a story that he had been robbed. Hsi-liu found out and was having him beaten almost to death when his elder brother Ch'ang-fu knelt at her feet and begged for mercy, offering to substitute his own body in his brother's place; so her anger gradually abated, but from that time on whenever Ch'ang-hu left the house his mother had him watched. This made his conduct slightly better, but the change did not really come from within his heart.

One day Ch'ang-hu asked his mother if he could join a group of merchants who were traveling to Loyang. In fact, he wanted to use this chance of a distant journey to give full scope to his desires, and was deeply worried that his mother might not agree to his request. But when Hsi-liu heard it she seemed to have no suspicions at all, gave him thirty taels of silver, and packed his baggage for him. And as he was leaving she handed him an ingot of gold, saying, "This has been handed down from our ancestors and is not for ordinary spending; keep it as ballast in your baggage and use it only in an emergency. Besides, this is your first experience of life on the road, and I am not expecting you to make any great profit; all I ask is that you not squander this thirty taels." She repeated this as Ch'ang-hu was leaving; he agreed completely and went on his way, elated and thoroughly pleased with himself.

When he reached Loyang he parted from his traveling companions with thanks and went to lodge in the house of a famous courtesan named Li; after passing ten nights or more with her, he had spent all his cash, but since he still had the gold ingot in his baggage, he didn't worry much about having run out of money. But when he took out the ingot and cut into it, he found it was fake gold; he was badly frightened and the color left his face. Li's mother, when she learned of the situation, cursed him sharply. Ch'ang-hu was deeply worried, for his purse was empty and there was nowhere for him to go; his only hope was that the girl would remember the happiness they had enjoyed together and would not cut him off right away. Suddenly two men came into his room with ropes which they fastened swiftly round his neck. Ch'ang-hu was terrified and had no idea what to do; when he piteously begged to know the reason for this treatment, he learned that the girl had taken the fake gold and lodged a complaint with the local prefect. Brought before the official, Ch'ang-hu was not allowed to testify but was put in fetters and beaten until he was nearly dead and then thrown into prison. Since he had no money for his expenses, he was badly mistreated by the jailers; by begging for food from his fellow prisoners he was just able to stay alive.

Now on the day that Ch'ang-hu had left home, his mother, Hsi-liu, had said to his elder brother, Ch'ang-fu, "Remember that when twenty days have passed I must send you off to Loyang. I have so many things to do that I'm afraid I might forget." Ch'ang-fu asked her what she meant, but she appeared overcome with grief and he withdrew, not daring to question her further. When the twenty days were up, he asked her again and she answered sadly, "Your younger brother is now leading a dissolute life, just as you did when you refused to study. If I had not acquired this terrible reputation, how would you ever have become what you are today? Everyone says that I am cruel, but none of them know of the tears that have flowed over my pillow." And the tears coursed down Hsi-liu's face while Ch'ang-fu stood respectfully waiting, not daring to inquire further. When she had finished weeping, Hsi-liu continued, "Since a dissolute heart still beat in your brother's body, I gave him some fake gold so that he would be badly mistreated. By now he must already be locked in prison. The governor thinks well of you; go and ask him for clemency so that your brother will be spared from death and a true sense of remorse be born in him."

Ch'ang-fu departed immediately; by the time he reached Lo-yang it was three days since his younger brother had been arrested; when he visited him in prison, his brother was desperate, his face like a ghost's. Ch'ang-hu wept when he saw his elder brother and could not raise his head. Ch'ang-fu wept also. Now since Ch'ang-fu was especially admired by the governor of the province, his name was known to everyone around, and when the prefect learned that he was Ch'ang-hu's elder brother, he immediately ordered Ch'ang-hu released from prison.

When Ch'ang-hu reached home he was still afraid his mother would be angry with him, so he came up to her, crawling on his knees. "Have you satisfied your desires?" she asked. Ch'ang-hu's face was still tear-stained; he dared make no further sound. Ch'ang-fu knelt at his side, and the mother at last told them both to rise.

From this time on Ch'ang-hu was deeply repentant and handled all the business of the household with diligence; if it happened that he was remiss over something, his mother would ask him to correct it without getting angry. Yet several months went by and still she did not speak to him about his working in trade; he wanted to ask her but did not dare, so he told his elder brother of his wishes. Hsi-liu was happy when she heard about it; she pawned some of her possessions and gave the money to Ch'ang-hu; within six months he had doubled the capital. That same year, in the autumn, Ch'ang-fu passed the provincial exams; three years later he obtained the highest degree. By this time his younger brother had made tens of thousands in trade.

A local merchant, on his way to Loyang, managed to sneak

a look at Hsi-liu. Though she was in her forties, she looked like a woman only a little over thirty; her clothes, her hair style were of the simplest. One would have thought she came from a poor family.

In Hsi-liu's story, though money produces the climax, lack of money is not the crux of the matter. That, rather, lies in the tangled tensions between compassion, discipline, and the misguided but still potent force of public opinion. But in other stories P'u Sung-ling showed how neighbors and relatives could descend on a widow and strip her home and family to the bones—whittling away the land by lawsuits or by physical coercion, harassing the widow with their attentions, driving her heirs into sexual excess or inducing them to gamble away their inheritances.

In T'an-ch'eng, too, we can find evidence of the financial pressure that widows were sometimes subjected to, though this is often confusingly couched in terms of pressure to remarry. Thus in the *Local History*'s brief biography of widow Wu, who had been left with a one-year-old baby, we find this passage: "After her mother-in-law also died, her late husband's elder brother tried to make her remarry. Woman Wu cut off her hair and disfigured her face, and finally returned her former possessions to her husband's elder brother, while she took her orphaned son back with her to her mother's home, and the boy was adopted into her clan." The death of the widow An is described in these terms: "She had been married for only half a year when her husband was overtaken by a violent illness and died. She wept in deep grief and vowed she would die with him; but the people in her district did not believe her. The following day she took her bride's trousseau and her other clothes and burned them. Her father-in-law and mother-in-law could not stop her. The members of the clan gathered, and examined her. Woman An beat her breast and cried out again and again, 'Oh, husband, you have passed away and I shall follow you.' Shortly thereafter she threw herself into the fire, but was rescued by a neighbor's wife. Those looking after her kept a close eye on her, but the next day she managed to trick her mother-in-law into leaving the room, barred the door, and hanged herself. She was eighteen years old."

Finally, in the case of the widow Kao, whose husband had been killed in the 1643 sack of T'an-ch'eng, we read: "At this time the family property was all ruined, soldiers and bandits roamed the area, there was nowhere for people to live in peace, she suffered the loneliness and misery of being a weak woman with a young orphan son. Her clansmen tried to make her marry again, scheming thus to get hold of her property, but woman Kao disfigured her own face and swore she would die rather than remarry. Weeping, she stated her cause to the magistrate and swore she would not be of two hearts. At her husband's burial she grieved bitterly, and took no food for seven days. She taught her son to read so that he would not fall below the standards set by his father. Her difficulties took ten thousand forms, she struggled constantly to have enough money, but the harder things were, the more she was upright in conduct, and stayed thus for over thirty years; and her son grew up well, to be upright and principled like her."

It seems certain that in each of these cases the crisis that led to the outcome—abandonment of property for woman Wu, suicide for woman An, and appeal to the authorities by woman Kao—stemmed from one specific subclause in the *Legal Code of the Ch'ing* dealing with the rights of widows and the laws of inheritance. The *Code,* issued in the name of the state and constantly updated by the Board of Punishments in Peking, was not only concerned with overt criminal acts; it also provided the standard and authoritative interpretations of the rights and obligations of Chinese in all walks of life, and married couples were no exception. The relevant passage (listed in the *Code's* economic section) stated, "If a widow remarries, her husband's property, as well as the dowry that she originally brought with her, shall become the property of her former husband's family." The clause, originally intended to encourage a widow to stay true to her dead husband's memory, had an obvious negative effect if—far from encouraging her in her sentiments of loyalty—the husband's relatives pushed the widow to remarry against her will. They would not just be divesting themselves of the cost of her upkeep and of child care, but be gaining substantial profits as well.

This clause of the *Legal Code* helps to explain the pressures that were placed on woman P'eng in T'an-ch'eng during the spring and early summer of 1670. She fulfilled part of her obligations immediately by enrolling her son, Lien, in the village school; it was only a small school, and the teacher was a part-time one who had to supplement his income by working in his own fields, but this was an important first stage if Lien was to gain literati status and honor his father. But almost from the first her husband's relatives, instead of supporting her, began to harass her. The main villains were her son's second cousins, the three brothers Ch'en Kuo-lin, Ch'en Kuo-hsiang, and Ch'en Kuo-lien. The youngest of them took her ox and refused to return it; this was a serious act, since the ox was not only an essential animal for families with fields to plow but was also treasured evidence of a family's status, well looked after and tethered before the doorway to the house (when not at work) for all to see. After taking the ox, Ch'en Kuo-lien extorted three taels from woman P'eng. The middle brother, Ch'en Kuo-hsiang, moved uninvited into her house and tried to drive her out. The clan head, Ch'en San-fu, did not intervene to help her, and her own husband's adopted brother, Ch'en T'ai-hsiang, was also of no assistance. But if they were trying to force her to move away from the area or to find another husband so as to protect herself and her son, they failed completely. Woman P'eng vowed she would not leave her home, and had an angry confrontation with the cousin Ch'en Kuo-hsiang, who swore, "I'll make sure that no scrap of anything is left to you."

The *Legal Code* also contained this provision: "A woman whose husband dies shall inherit his property when there is no son to receive it; but in such cases the clan head must choose an heir to inherit the property in accordance with the degrees of family relationship." From Ch'en Kuo-hsiang's threat, and from his later actions, it is clear that he knew at least the general outlines of this provision and that he intended to try to take advantage of it. For if the boy Lien was dead, and the letter of the law was observed, the three brothers would inherit the property, since the Ch'en family tree had this form in 1670:

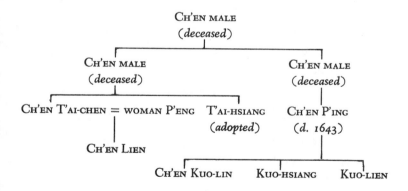

Ch'en Lien's uncle, T'ai-hsiang, could not inherit, according to the law, because he had been adopted in from another lineage, by a father who already possessed a natural son, and thus was not entitled to take precedence over males in the direct line of Ch'en ancestral descent where matters of inheritance were concerned.

The problem for the three Ch'en brothers then became

this: how to kill the boy Ch'en Lien and receive only a minimal penalty so that they could live to inherit the property. It was Ch'en Kuo-hsiang who came up with an answer, an answer that depended for its success on the chaos of recent events in T'an-ch'eng county and (once again) on some familiarity with the law. The brothers' father, Ch'en P'ing, like so many others, had died when the Manchu troops sacked T'an-ch'eng in 1643; but his corpse had never been recovered, and the exact cause and place of death were unknown. Ch'en Kuo-hsiang decided to invent a story that his father had been killed by Ch'en Lien's father; that as a filial son he had seethed with rage over this event; and that he had finally avenged his dead father by killing—not the murderer, because the murderer was dead—but the closest relative, the murderer's own son. To explain this act of filial vengeance after almost thirty years had passed since his father's death, he would claim that he had been drinking heavily just before taking action.

There was indeed a vengeance clause concerning sons and their parents in the *Legal Code of the Ch'ing*, though the Ch'ens did not have all the details right. The actual stipulations were these: "Whenever a grandparent or parent is being attacked by an assailant, and the grandson or son *immediately* intervenes to protect him and attacks the assailant in return, if the son or grandson causes no injury, he shall receive no punishment; if he causes injury, he shall be punished in accordance with the laws on assault, lessened by three degrees; if he causes death, he shall be punished as in regular cases of homicide.

"If a grandparent or parent is killed by an assailant, and the son or grandson, without reporting the matter to the authorities, acts on his own initiative and kills the murderer, he shall be beaten sixty strokes; if he kills the murderer *immediately*, he shall receive no punishment."

Officials of the Board of Punishments had noted the importance of the word "immediately" in both these clauses and had inserted a brief modifier to it in 1646: if the son or grandson acted not "immediately" but "after a slight delay," then he should be punished in accordance with the regular laws on assault or (in the case of murdering the parent's murderer) in accordance with the laws on "killing without authority a person who merits the death penalty," that is to say, with a beating of one hundred blows.

The Ch'en brothers were not aware of the finer points of this law, and they assumed that "sons avenging a father's death" could generally expect to receive lenient treatment from the authorities. In fact, this had been true in earlier periods of Chinese history, and it was to control such acts of vengeance that the *Code* had taken the precise stand then in force. The brothers did not realize that the law would neither accept twenty-seven years as a reasonable period of elapsed time nor accept the son of the murderer as an adequate substitute for the murderer himself.

On July 6, 1670, the middle of the three brothers, Ch'en Kuo-hsiang, walked to the schoolhouse in T'an-ch'eng where the boy Ch'en Lien was studying with his schoolmates. He carried with him a heavy wooden paddle, of the kind used to beat loads of washing. The teacher was absent. Ch'en Kuo-hsiang sat down on the desk and asked the children where their teacher was. They replied that he was out in his fields, working. Ch'en Kuo-hsiang then seized Lien and dragged him out of the schoolroom. The schoolroom was on the edge of the temple compound, and it was in front of the temple to the goddess of mercy, Kuan-yin, that he beat the boy to death.

The next morning Ch'en Kuo-hsiang handed himself over to the authorities, admitting responsibility for the murder, but claiming that he had acted out of filial love and while under the influence of drink. He said he had run into Ch'en Lien by chance in the temple, and the meeting had triggered the act of revenge. His case collapsed almost instantly, since the school-boys said he had been sober when he came to the classroom, and had begun beating Ch'en Lien in their sight. Further-more, the three brothers gave conflicting testimony as to where their father had allegedly been murdered by Ch'en T'ai-chen those many years ago, and they could produce no wit-nesses who had ever heard them speak of vengeance before the summer of 1670. Indeed, the evidence showed that they had lived in harmony with their father's alleged murderer for nearly thirty years. As the magistrate sarcastically remarked, it was fortunate for Ch'en T'ai-chen that for almost thirty years he had never met his nephew while the nephew was drunk.

Ch'en Kuo-hsiang was, therefore, tried not under the filial piety vengeance substatutes, as he had hoped, but under quite a different section of the *Code,* that of "striking a relative in the second, third, or fourth degree." It was the magistrate's opinion that in view of the relationship between the murderer and victim the charge should be "beating to death a relation of the third degree"; thus whether or not Ch'en Kuo-hsiang was junior or senior to Lien, since he had killed by design, convic-tion brought the penalty of strangulation.

Woman P'eng did not get her ox or her money back, be-cause the younger of the three brothers, who had taken them, fled across the border from T'an-ch'eng and could not be found. Since her boy was dead, and she was now left with no male relations in direct line of descent to her husband, the clan head was ordered to nominate a member of another branch of the Ch'en clan to be her heir.

Four

THE
FEUD

P'u SUNG-LING knew all about family quarrels. This is how he described his own early married life:

I was my father's third son, and over ten years old before I was engaged. My parents heard that a Mr. Liu was ready to betroth his second daughter, and so began to negotiate through a matchmaker. When people criticized my father for his poverty, Mr. Liu answered, "I hear that he is like those immortals who endure humiliation on earth; also that he teaches his sons to read, and has not given up working despite his poverty. He will make sure that they do not go astray, so what does it matter that he is poor?" So they drew up the contract. In 1655 rumors spread around that the Court was going to choose girls from good families to be imperial concubines, and everyone grew very uneasy. At first Mr. Liu did not believe this, but he did not dare be stubborn, so he went along with everyone else and sent his daughter to live in his son-in-law's house. She was twelve at the time and slept in the same room as her future mother-in-law, woman Tung. When the rumors died down she returned to her own home.

Two years later we were married. She was affectionate, artless in speech, and not garrulous; and if she was not as bright as her sisters-in-law, neither was she unpleasant to her mother-in-law, as they were. My mother used to say that my wife had the heart of a newborn baby; she was very fond of her, favored her, and would praise her to all comers. This served to annoy the wife of my eldest brother more than ever; she ganged up with the other sisters-in-law against my wife, blamed my mother for her favoritism, and continually snooped around her. But my mother continued to act honorably and justly, protecting my wife with her love as if she were one of my mother's own children—she had done the same with the concubine's son—and never giving the smallest cause for reproach.

Nevertheless, the other sisters-in-law used the silliest pretexts to find fault with my mother; they caused an endless uproar and their long tongues were never still. At last my father said, "Things can't go on like this any longer," and divided his half dozen acres of land among his sons. It was a bad year, and we got no more than five measures of buckwheat and three of millet. The others refused to take any implements that were broken and squabbled over getting ones that were still in good condition, but my wife remained speechless, as if she were dumb. My brothers all ended up with separate dwellings in the main compound, each of which had a kitchen and sitting room in perfect condition. I was the only one who had to move out altogether, and ended up in an old peasant cottage of three rooms, where not one wall was whole; small trees grew dense around it, and everything was covered with a tangle of thorns and weeds.

From these experiences P'u Sung-ling developed some of his most savage stories: in one of these a large family of brothers and stepbrothers—each named after an impeccable Confucian virtue—tear their family apart in a series of increasingly bitter fights. From his observation of local bandit groups, moreover, and from prevalent local tales, he moved beyond pastiche to see the effects of raw terror within a community and the ways that misery spawned recklessness and sudden, unreasoning violence that were almost impossible to deal with. P'u Sung-ling had little faith in local officials' ability to handle situations of this sort, and the moral of the following story about Ts'ui Meng was merely that such violence must ultimately be controlled by the individual's will; if channeled for the good of the community there was then a hope that it might ultimately help to make up for the officials' neglect and enable the local villagers to protect themselves.

Ts'ui Meng, "Ts'ui the violent"—who had the alternate name Wu-meng, "nonviolent"—was the son of a distinguished family in Chien-ch'ang. His character was tough and unyielding, and even when he was a child in school, if one of his classmates slightly contradicted him about something, he would fly at him, hitting and beating. His teacher kept trying to stop him, but without success, and so gave him his name, and his alternate name.

By the time Ts'ui was sixteen or seventeen he had incredible martial strength, and seizing a long pole, he could vault onto the high roof of a house. He delighted in correcting injustices, and so everyone in his district respected him; the petitioners seeking his help crowded the stairs and filled the rooms of his house. Ts'ui curbed the violent people and assisted the weak, and did not mind if he made some people hate him. If someone opposed him, Ts'ui would strike him with stones or a staff, and they would end up badly hurt; so whenever his anger began to rise, no one dared to try to control him.

Only to his mother did Ts'ui show respect, and he would calm down when she appeared: she would scold him for his conduct, and he would respond obediently to all her commands, but as soon as she was gone he would forget all about it.

In the next-door house lived a vicious wife who cruelly mistreated her mother-in-law, so that the old lady had almost died
from hunger. The old lady's son used to feed her in secret, but
when the wife found out about it she cursed the old woman on
every pretext; the yelling could be heard by all the neighboring
households. Ts'ui was enraged; he climbed over the wall into the
woman's house, cut off her nose and ears, her lips and tongue, and
left her dead. Ts'ui's mother was greatly alarmed when she heard
what had happened; she called the neighbor over and did everything she could to comfort him. She also gave him a young slave
girl, and so the whole business was hushed up.

But now Ts'ui's mother wept and would eat no food. He was
worried in turn. He knelt before her and begged to be beaten;
he told her that he was deeply sorry. His mother wept on and
made no reply till Ts'ui's wife, Chou, knelt down at his side; then
the mother beat her son, and besides that she took a needle and
punctured his forearm with it in the form of two crossed lines,
rubbing red earth into the marks so that they could never be
erased. Ts'ui endured all this, and when it was done his mother
began to eat again.

Ts'ui's mother delighted in offering food to Buddhist and
Taoist mendicants, and they would come by her house and eat
their fill. One day Ts'ui encountered a Taoist monk in her doorway, and the monk gazed at him, saying, "Your honor has the
air of one who is going to meet with the gravest misfortune, and
I fear it will be difficult to assure you of a natural end. It should
not be thus in the household of those who have given themselves to good works."

Ts'ui had only just received the warning from his mother, and
so when he heard these words he replied respectfully, "I am quite
aware of that, but whenever I see a case of injustice, there is no
way I can hold myself back. If I force myself to change, would
I be able to avoid this fate?"

"Don't let us talk of avoiding or not avoiding things for the moment," the Taoist answered with a smile. "First I would like you to ask yourself whether you can change or not. You will have to battle painfully with yourself, but if there is one chance in ten thousand that you can do it, then I shall impart to you the skills for avoiding death." Ts'ui had never had any belief in exorcism, so he merely smiled and made no reply. "I can tell you are not a believer," said the monk, "but what I am talking about has nothing to do with magical practices. The operation involves the highest level of virtue, and if it does not succeed no damage will have been done." So Ts'ui asked to be enlightened further, and the monk replied, "Outside your door there is a youngster with whom you must form a close friendship; when you are condemned to death it is he who will be able to restore your life to you." And he called Ts'ui to come outside, and pointed out the person he meant.

The boy was surnamed Chao; his given name was Seng-ko. The Chao family were originally from Nan-ch'ang, but since there had been a year of bad famine there, they had moved to Chien-ch'ang. From this time on Ts'ui showed the greatest affection for Chao Seng-ko; he invited him to live with him at home and gave him everything that he could require. Chao Seng-ko was twelve years old at this time; he paid his formal respects to Ts'ui's mother and was adopted as his younger brother. The following year the head of the Chao family, having affairs to attend to in the east, departed with all his family, so Ts'ui lost all contact with Seng-ko.

Ever since the death of the wife in the next-door house, Ts'ui's mother had kept a tight watch over her son; and if anyone came by to tell him his troubles, she would send that person away without ceremony. One day the younger brother of Ts'ui's mother died, and Ts'ui went along with her to pay their respects to the bereaved family. On the road they came upon a group of people escorting a young man in bonds; they were swearing at him to hurry up, and hitting him. The crowd of those watching what was going on had blocked the road, and none of the travelers could get by. Ts'ui asked what was happening, and those who recognized him clustered around him to explain.

What had happened was this: There was the son of a certain well-known member of the gentry who tyrannized his whole district; having noticed the beauty of Li Shen's wife, he determined to have her for himself. Since he had no direct way to do this, he sent off one of his household retainers to get into a gambling game with Li Shen; as they played he lent Li large sums of money at high interest, saying he could post his wife as bond for the loans, and the more Li lost the more he gave him, until by morning Li had run up debts of several thousand taels. By the time half a year had gone by, principal and interest came to over thirty thousand taels, and there was no way Li could pay it back. So they sent over a group of men to seize his wife by force, and when Li wept and protested outside their gateway, they dragged him off and tied him to a tree, beating him and jabbing him with spikes until he was forced to sign a statement that he would not pursue the matter further.

When Ts'ui heard this he felt the fury rising up inside him like a mountain—he whipped his horse forward as if he were about to do battle. But opening the curtains of her sedan chair, his mother cried out, "Hey! Are you going to start that again?" and Ts'ui stopped. After they had made their condolences they returned home, but Ts'ui would neither speak nor eat; he sat motionless, staring straight ahead, as if angered by something. His wife asked him what was the matter, but he would not answer. That night he lay on the bed fully clothed and tossed and turned till morning; the next night he did the same. Suddenly he rose and left the room; as abruptly he returned and lay down again. This he did three or four times, his wife did not dare question him; she just lay anxiously, listening. Finally Ts'ui went out for some time; when he returned he closed the door and fell into a deep sleep.

That same night somebody killed the wife stealer as he lay on his bed—his stomach was ripped open so that his intestines spilled out, and Li's wife was also found, naked and dead, on the floor by the bed.

The local officials suspected Li himself of the crime and had him arrested; they tortured him terribly with the pressing boards until the bones of his ankles showed through the skin, but still he would not confess. Finally after more than a year he could bear the punishment no more: he made a false confession and was condemned to death.

At this time Ts'ui's mother died, and when the funeral was over, Ts'ui said to his wife, "It was indeed I who killed that man, but because my old mother was still alive I did not dare admit it. Now that my service to her is over, how can I let someone else take the blame for a crime that I myself committed? I must report to the officials and meet my death." Ts'ui's wife was terrified and clung to him, but he tore himself from her grasp and departed, handing himself in to the yamen. The magistrate was greatly surprised and had Ts'ui put in prison, planning to free Li; but Li would not leave, insisting that he really was the guilty one. The magistrate could not decide the case and kept them both in custody. Li's relatives all came to argue with him, but he said, "What Ts'ui did was what I wanted to do but was unable to. After he had done this for me, how could I bear to sit back and watch him die? I am going to act as if Ts'ui had never handed himself in." He refused to retract his confession, and fought with Ts'ui over it, until finally everyone at the yamen learned the true story and Li was forced to leave the prison. Ts'ui was condemned to death.

Just before the date for his execution an official from the Board of Punishments named Chao happened to be in the area inspecting the lists of prisoners condemned for capital crimes, to see if any might deserve a reduction in sentence. When he came upon Ts'ui's name he set aside the others and called for him. Ts'ui entered, looked up to the platform where the official was sitting, and recognized Chao Seng-ko! Both grieved and happy, he told him the true story; Chao paced back and forth for a long time, and then ordered Ts'ui kept in prison, but told the jailers to treat him well. Chao then reduced his sentence in accordance with the procedures for those who have turned themselves in and confessed, and had him sent into exile to serve as a soldier in Yunnan. Li enrolled himself as Ts'ui's servant and went with him. Before a year had passed he received an amnesty and returned home; this again was due to Chao's influence.

After Ts'ui returned home, Li stayed always with him and undertook the management of all his business affairs. When Ts'ui offered him money, Li would not accept it; he took special delight in mastering the skills of pole climbing and boxing, and Ts'ui treated him with great consideration, buying a wife for him and giving him lands. Ts'ui now used all his strength to change his former conduct, and every time he would touch the scars on his forearm his eyes shone with tears; if quarrels broke out among their neighbors in the district, Li would pretend that he had been told to act as peacemaker, and then kept the matter concealed from Ts'ui.

There was a certain student of the Imperial Academy named Wang whose family was overbearing and rich; everyone from round about who was untrustworthy or immoral used to gather at the Wangs' home. As for the substantial local families, many of them were ravaged, and if they tried to protest, Wang would send brigands to kill them on the road. Wang's son was as licentious and cruel as his father, and the two of them maintained an illicit relationship with a widowed aunt of Wang's. Wang's own wife, woman Ch'iu, tried to get him to stop, and he strangled her; so woman Ch'iu's brothers lodged a formal complaint with the magistrate. Wang, however, bribed the magistrate, and the Ch'iu brothers were charged in turn with lodging a false charge. The brothers, not knowing where to turn, went to Ts'ui to beg for help, but Li intercepted them and made them go away.

A few days later some guests came by, and since there happened to be no servants around, Ts'ui told Li Shen to go and prepare the tea. Li stayed silent and left the room; later he said to someone, "I am a friend of Ts'ui Meng, I followed him ten thousand *li* into exile, you cannot say I have not behaved well; whereas he has never paid me wages and treats me as if I were his servant. I don't like that." And he left angrily. The person told Ts'ui of this conversation, and he was surprised at the change in Li, though he did nothing about it.

Without warning Li laid an accusation against Ts'ui in the magistrate's court, charging him with having paid him no wages for three years. Ts'ui was completely astonished and went off in person to confront him; Li argued angrily with him, but the magistrate was not convinced by Li and had him beaten and dismissed from the court. A few days after this Li suddenly broke into Wang's house at night and killed the father, the son, and the aunt; he stuck a piece of paper to the wall on which he wrote his name, but when the constables came to arrest him they found he had disappeared without a trace. The surviving members of the Wang family suspected that Ts'ui had been the person responsible, but the magistrate did not believe them. Only then did Ts'ui begin to understand that Li had made his previous accusation so that Ts'ui would not be involved in this later killing. Warrants were sent around to the nearby counties ordering the arrest of Li, but since at this time Li Tzu-ch'eng's rebellion* was raging, the whole business was forgotten about; and after the Ming dynasty fell, Li Shen returned home with his family and resumed his friendship with Ts'ui, as before.

At this time bands of robbers sprang up everywhere, and a nephew of Wang's named Wang Te-jen assembled a group of toughs who had once been in league with his uncle; they took

* Li Tzu-ch'eng raised a rebel army in northwest China in the 1630s and seized Peking in 1644, ending the Ming dynasty. He was ousted the same year by the Manchus, who formed the Ch'ing dynasty.

a base in the mountains and became thieves, pillaging the villages and grazing grounds in the area. One night he assembled the band and came down, saying that he would be revenged on Ts'ui. Ts'ui happened to be away from home, and Li Shen luckily saw them coming and was able to escape over the wall and hide in a safe place. The robbers searched for Ts'ui, and when they could not find him they took his wife and any objects of value that were there, then left.

When Li got back only one servant remained, and he was too frightened and upset to know what to do. Li took a length of rope and cut it into dozens of pieces; he gave the shorter pieces to the servant and kept the longer ones for himself. He told the servant to go beyond the robbers' lair and climb halfway up the mountain, where he was to set fire to the bits of rope and scatter them among the patches of briers; then he could return home, with nothing more to worry about. The servant agreed to do what he asked, and went off on his mission. Li had noticed that the robbers all wore red sashes round their waists and red turbans on their heads, so he dressed himself in the same fashion. Outside the gateway was an old mare that had just foaled and had been left there by the robbers; Li tethered the foal and saddled the horse, put the bit in its mouth, and set off. When he reached the robbers' lair, which was in a large village they had captured, he tethered the mare outside the village and climbed in over the wall. He saw crowds of robbers moving around everywhere, still carrying their arms; and by skillful questioning he was able to find out that Ts'ui's wife was being kept in Wang's house. Shortly thereafter the signal was given for everyone to retire for the night, and they were just rumbling off to obey when someone called out that there was a fire in the eastern hills; all the robbers gathered to watch. At first there were only one or two specks of light, but more and more appeared like stars; Li rushed up breathlessly, shouting out that there was danger in the eastern hills. Wang was alarmed, put on his armor, and led off his troops, while Li slipped away from the group to the right and made his way back into the village.

He saw two of the robbers standing guard under an awning, and said to them, "General Wang forgot his sword." As they hurried in to look for it Li struck at their heads from behind: one of them fell dead, the other turned around to look at Li, who beheaded him as well. Carrying Ts'ui's wife on his back, Li climbed over the wall, untied the horse, and gave the reins to the woman, saying, "Since you don't know the way back, just let the horse find it." The mare hurried off at a trot, anxious to get back to her foal. Li followed on after them until he reached a defile in the mountains; there he set fire to the pieces of rope, which he had hung up in various places, and returned home.

Next day Ts'ui returned; because of the gross insult he had suffered he was torn body and soul with impetuous rage and wanted to ride out alone to attack the bandits, but Li was able to dissuade him. They assembled all the villagers to make a common strategy, but most of them were timorous and did not dare take action; after discussing the problem from every point of view, they found about twenty villagers who seemed brave enough, though unfortunately they had no weapons. It happened at this time that they caught two spies in the home of Wang Te-jen's relatives, and Ts'ui was just about to kill them when Li stopped him; he told the twenty villagers to pick up simple wooden poles and line up in front of the two robbers, then cut off the bandits' ears and let them go. The villagers were all angry, and said to Li, "We were afraid that the bandits would find out we had no other weapons than these, and now you have shown them. If they come back with the whole band, the entire village will be unprotected."

"I want them to come," said Li. First he seized and killed those who had been sheltering the bandits, and then he sent men all around to get bows and arrows and firearms while he himself went to the city and borrowed two large cannon.

At nightfall Li Shen took the strongest villagers with him to the defile in the mountains and put the cannon in position, leaving two men there with concealed fire and telling them to shoot when they saw the bandits. Then he went to the defile at the eastern end of the valley, cut down a number of trees, and piled them on the top of the slope; he and Ts'ui each took ten men and waited at the edge of the cliff. Near the end of the first watch they heard the sound of horses neighing in the distance, and the bandits arrived, riding past in an unbroken stream. The villagers waited until all the bandits had entered the valley, then sent the trees rolling down to cut their retreat; at the same moment the cannon opened fire, and the sounds of the men crying out rose in the air, filling the mountains and valleys. The bandits fled back, trampling each other, but when they reached the entrance to the valley in the east they could not get through, and there was no other means of escape. From both cliffs arrows and shot rained down; robbers with severed heads and shattered limbs lay piled in confusion on the valley floor.

Only some twenty robbers were left alive, and they knelt long on the ground, begging for their lives; men were sent down to tie them up, and they were brought back as prisoners. Profiting from the victory, the villagers went to the bandits' lair, but the guards heard them coming and escaped into hiding; so the villagers took away all the military supplies from the camp and returned home.

Ts'ui was overjoyed and asked Li to explain his earlier plan of lighting the fires. Li replied, "I had the servant light the fires at the eastern mountains because I feared the bandits might pursue me to the west; I used short pieces of rope because I wanted them to burn through quickly, fearing that the bandits' scouts might find out that there was no one there. I placed the fires at the entrance to the valley because the entrance was narrow and could be blocked off by one person; if the bandits got there in pursuit of me, they would be frightened back when they saw the fires. It was a clumsy plan, designed for a moment of extreme danger." They questioned some of the captured robbers, who confirmed that they pursued Li into the valley but were frightened when they saw the fires, and withdrew.

They cut off the noses and ears of the twenty bandits, and then let them go. From this time forth the fame of the two men spread around, and all those from near and far who were fleeing from disasters came to be their followers, crowding around as on a market day. The two formed a local defense force of more than three hundred men, and not one of the cruel bandits in the area dared to attack them; the people of the region trusted in the two men, and lived in peace.

In T'an-ch'eng county there lived a Wang family that could have been the prototype for P'u Sung-ling's fictional Wangs. The family head was a certain Wang San, who had originally lived in the area of Ch'i-hsia county, two hundred and fifty miles to the northeast; he had been a subcommander in the army of Yü Ch'i, the rebel who had held out for months against three Manchu armies in the Shantung mountains during 1661 and early 1662. When the rebels were broken by the besieging armies and by the savage reprisals taken against the villages near their base areas, Yü Ch'i had managed to escape, leaving many of his subordinates behind to be executed; Wang San had escaped at the same time, and he made his way to T'an-ch'eng. There, with the money he brought with him, he had purchased a fortified farm house in Wu-chang village, situated in the very south of the county, so that in an emergency he could leave the jurisdiction of Shantung by slipping across the border at P'ei into Kiangsu province. The villagers had seen groups of horsemen ride up to his house at night armed with swords and bows, and often the Wangs rode off for days on end; but no one had dared to report the family to the authorities.

Wang San had a son as tough as he was, named Wang K'o-hsi, who had married the daughter of a local landlord named Chiang; that same Chiang had deeded sixty acres of good land to the Wangs in addition to letting his daughter enter their family. Chiang's motive in both these transactions was to buy protection from the Wangs—for everyone in the area knew that the Wangs were gangsters as well as landlords.

T'an-ch'eng presented no prototype for P'u Sung-ling's fictional hero, the violent Ts'ui Meng; perhaps a local farmer named Li Tung-chen came the nearest of anyone to catching a flicker of the same independence. Li lived fifteen miles southwest of T'an-ch'eng city, near Lao-kou market, where he owned a sprawling home—several rooms with earth walls and floors grouped around a central courtyard, surrounded by a wall. It was a poor sort of house despite its size, with nothing worth stealing. Six of his seven sons lived there with him—his eldest son, Li Yüan, had moved a short distance, to Ni-hu village, and set up on his own.

Father and eldest son had both been hoping to obtain a lease on the sixty acres of land owned by Chiang, since it abutted on theirs—their "mouths had been watering for it," according to the neighbors—and they were furious when Chiang, in the spring of 1670, deeded the land to Wang San. The Lis showed their disappointment that Chiang had made his land over to Wang by being careless about where their animals strayed: several times their donkeys and pigs crossed the boundaries of Wang's new fields.

One day in early summer Wang K'o-hsi came with men to work on his land and found one of Li Yüan's pigs rooting there. He killed the pig and cursed out Li Tung-chen for letting his animals trample the Wang fields. Li Tung-chen, enraged in turn, swore that the Wangs were the "leaders of a gang of mounted thugs." Though it was true enough, the Wangs decided this last charge was an act of public defiance that could not be forgiven; and on July 6 (the day, by coincidence, on which Ch'en Kuo-hsiang beat Ch'en Lien to death near the city) they met in their home with three friends to plan their reprisal for Li's insult. They decided to recruit two more men—Su Ta, famous for his pugnacity, and Li the Fat, experienced and shrewd; and they sent one of their number to the diviner to find out what would be a lucky day to "undertake a great matter." The diviner recommended the day "Double Six," the sixth day of the sixth lunar month (July 22), so the Wangs laid their plans for that evening.

On the afternoon of the twenty-second, Wang's group rode across country on donkeys, carrying concealed weapons; they left the donkeys on the hill behind Li Tung-chen's house and hid in the underbrush there until darkness fell. There were eight of them altogether: one stayed to guard the donkeys; Wang San covered the road behind the house; two were sent to watch the front entrance; Wang K'o-hsi, his face smeared with red mud to avoid recognition, climbed with the three others over the wall into Li Tung-chen's courtyard. It was a hot night, and Li was lying out in the courtyard with two friends and several of his sons. Before he could rise, Wang K'o-hsi speared him in the stomach; as Li staggered to his feet, crying out, "Who's here?" a sword blow caught him on the back of the neck, another pierced his side, and he fell dead. Li's fifth son was killed next. Then his seventh. The sixth son ran for the gate, but was cut down. (He died the next day.) The women were left unharmed, but the two guests were both wounded and were being forced to tell Wang where the other sons were when the third son, who was still able to run despite a wound in his head, reached a neighbor's house and rang an alarm bell. At the sound of the bell the killers regrouped and rode back home.

For three days the surviving members of the Li family tried to decide what to do. None of them dared to accuse the

Wangs directly; nor did the neighbors; nor did the wounded guests. The Lis finally decided to bring a double charge of "robbery out of vengeance, and the murder of four persons in one family" against Chiang, the neighbor who had given his land to the Wangs; the Lis calculated that in order to clear himself of the charges Chiang would have to end up by implicating the Wangs. But though the magistrate's constables did arrest Chiang in response to the Lis' charge and bring him into T'an-ch'eng city for questioning, no one had anticipated the extent of Wang San's gall: Wang came in person to the court, swore out a statement that Chiang was an honest person, that there was no cause to arrest him, and that he, Wang, would stand guarantor for Chiang's conduct. With that he escorted him out of the court under the astonished gaze of the courtroom clerks, none of whom dared protest.

Two weeks later Li Yüan lodged another charge, this time of "homicide of four persons," dropping the references to vengeance and robbery and naming nobody as the accused. Huang Liu-hung, who had just taken up office as magistrate, decided to try to find out what lay behind these various accusations, though he knew it would be difficult, since security, even in his own office, was poor. He had located at least twenty-four local ruffians, scattered across the four districts of his county, all of whom had contacts at different levels within his own yamen and got news of any decision as soon as he made it.

The magistrate's method was to proceed by indirection. He first summoned Li Yüan to a private nighttime interview, during which he persuaded him to name the protagonists in the case by promising to help his family attain their vengeance on the killers. Once Li had named the Wangs and provided details of the killings, Huang sent him home. The next day he summoned the one police constable he was sure he could trust, Yü Piao, and asked him, "Do you know the names of the robbers who killed Li Tung-chen and his sons?"

Yü stared at him in alarm for some time, and replied, "Though I know who it is, I dare not tell you the name."

Huang: "Then just tell me how we can catch him."

Yü: "The difficulty would not be in catching him, but I'm afraid he'd get advance news of it."

Huang: "Can you think of anyone who would like to be revenged on this robber?"

Yü Piao again thought for a long time, and answered, "There's a man in this county called Kuan Ming-yü whose younger brother was killed by the robber; every time he talks about it he is moved to tears, but he doesn't know how to take his revenge."

Huang continued to move carefully, since the mere summoning of this Kuan might lay him open to reprisals. Instead, he summoned Kuan's cousin Kuan Ming-pao, who was involved in a criminal case, and had him accompanied to the hearing by Kuan Ming-yü, in his capacity as village headman. After the hearing he summoned Kuan Ming-yü to a private interview, and again proceeded by question and answer:

Huang: "Is that Ming-pao your younger brother?"

Kuan: "No, he's my younger cousin."

Huang: "Are you an only child, with no younger brother?"

Kuan: "I had a younger brother, but he's dead."

Huang: "How did he die?"

Kuan: "He was killed by robbers."

Huang: "Which robbers?"

Kuan: "Since your honor asks me that, he must surely know who it was. The killer of my brother was Wang San. My brother was thirteen years old, and while out cutting grain accidentally stepped over the line onto Wang San's land. Wang San tied him up, dragged him to his home, killed him and buried his body somewhere in the garden behind his house. I dare not tell you how much I still hate him. The man who killed Li Tung-chen and his sons was the same Wang San. If your honor has any assignment for me, you have only to tell me."

Huang: "You'll have a chance to avenge your brother's death. The day after tomorrow I'll be coming to check levies in the eastern district. Early on that morning you must pay a visit to Wang San and make sure he is indeed at home; I'll tell Yü Piao to be hiding behind the garden wall, and as soon as you've told Yü, I will be there. If there are any leaks I shall have you killed."

Huang then took six taels of silver and gave Kuan three, promising him the rest after Wang San had been caught.

To keep his side of the bargain, the magistrate had to assemble a force which would be strong enough to arrest the Wangs, yet news of which would not reach them in advance. On paper, at least, he had enough troops to deal with the situation. There were three detachments of regular soldiers in T'an-ch'eng county: 150 soldiers were garrisoned in the county capital, and either used to defend the city or the smaller market towns out in the countryside; 80 were on duty at the southernmost point of the county, at the important post station of Hung-hua-fou; 21 were assigned to guard the seven government inns on the main roads. About a quarter of these troops were classified as cavalry, the rest as infantry. A further 132 riders and grooms were attached to the other main post stations. And the magistrate had his own personal staff of 103; among this number were 50 militia soldiers, 16 runners, and 8 police constables. These police constables seem to have been Huang Liu-hung's most reliable staff—at seventeen and a half taels a year they were paid almost three times as much as the runners and soldiers, who only earned six—and were well trained and loyal; but the others posed problems. There was no particular shared esprit: the soldiers and grooms were constantly feuding with each other, even brawling in the streets, while both troops and horsemen used violence against the clerks and runners. The horses were in terrible condition—there were nowhere near the stipulated number of 130, and many of those in the stables were too weak to be ridden. Even the lieutenant in charge of the city troops, Chu Ch'eng-ming, although he was brave enough and a good officer, could not be relied on in this case, since he was known to have been on friendly terms with the Wangs.

To minimize the chance of leaks, the magistrate simply announced that he would be going on a routine tour of inspection in the area around the market town of Ma-t'ou. The evening after his conversation with Kuan Ming-yü, he assembled a group of just under forty riders—the eight police constables and thirty of his own militia and staff—and set off for Ma-t'ou. When Lieutenant Chu offered to accompany him, Huang said that would not be necessary, but they could meet up the following day near the town of Chung-fang. To give his story credence, the magistrate and his men rode the six miles west to Ma-t'ou, through steady rain; but instead of staying there they left, after a short rest, and rode through the night southeast to Chung-fang, which they reached a little before dawn. Here, about six miles from the Wangs' house, they ate and rested, while the police constable Yü Piao checked in at his rendezvous with Kuan Ming-yü.

The group was still at breakfast when Yü Piao galloped back to say that Kuan Ming-yü had arrived as planned at Wang San's house, offering to pay his respects and bringing two geese as a present. Delighted, Wang San had asked him in, and the two had had some drinks together; but the magistrate would have to hurry, since Wang was planning to ride over to the market at Lao-kou later in the morning. Huang had just been joined by Lieutenant Chu with twenty more cavalry, yet even as they galloped off to Wang San's house he refused to tell Chu where they were going, shouting out, "You'll know when you get there."

Despite the elaborate precautions, Wang San had somehow been alerted by the time they arrived. The gates were barred; men, some with firearms, some with swords, were at their posts; and Wang San (identified by one of Huang's police constables) was standing in full view on the wall, holding a long halberd with a crescent blade.

Huang's main worry was that Wang's men would scatter out into the nearby fields of high kaoliang, and he knew it would take a difficult battle to storm the house. So when Wang made a feigned retreat toward the back of his house, Huang pretended to be taken in, and he led his own troops around to the back, hoping that if given the chance Wang would run for P'ei and that he might be able to trap him on the level ground near the border. "We entice the tiger to come down from the mountain," Huang told his police. As Wang and twenty of his men rode out through the front gate, Huang joined in pursuit; Wang was still ahead of his pursuers as they reached the P'ei border, and Lieutenant Chu reined in his troops, saying that it was against regulations to go beyond their jurisdiction. But Huang, letting the excitement of the chase get ahead of his usual administrator's caution, called out, "T'an troops are chasing T'an bandits—what have regulations got to do with it?" and rode his men over the river.

On the other bank, with their backs to a hill, Wang and his men were waiting for them. It is not clear why they stopped there: perhaps their horses were exhausted, perhaps they thought the T'an-ch'eng men would stop on their own side of the border, perhaps they thought the magistrate's men would have no stomach for a fight. The latter is the most likely, for Wang's men moved into the offensive at once, unhorsing one of Chu's squad commanders with their lances and striking another in the chest; these commanders, since they were wearing chest armor, were not badly hurt, but the examples discouraged anyone else from advancing until one of the magistrate's militia men hit one of Wang's men in the chest with an arrow and killed him. The militia men's spirits were further raised by the arrival of Kuan Ming-yü with around thirty armed villagers, so that the Wangs were now outnumbered nearly ninety to twenty, and the battle was sharply joined.

Wang K'o-hsi was knocked out by Kuan Ming-yü with his cudgel, and Wang San, riding to his son's rescue, was felled with an arrow in the chest. Three other of Wang's companions were killed or captured, and the rest escaped. Huang did not pursue them; he had captured the two Wangs, the men he wanted most.

The Wangs were taken back to T'an-ch'eng city and interrogated through the night. Wang San's arrow wound was festering, and he died during the questioning, though not before he admitted his part in the killing of Li Tung-chen. Wang K'o-hsi also confessed. Despite Wang San's death the city of T'an-ch'eng was in a panic. The gentry packed their possessions, fearing there might be a general rising of the Wangs' supporters; and Huang grew so anxious about an attempt being made to free Wang K'o-hsi from jail that he had him transported to the stronger prison in I-chou, to the north.

The day after the arrest of the Wangs, over eighty households fled from the villages in southeastern T'an-ch'eng. All were believed to have been connected with Wang San's gang, and presumably they now feared reprisals, but it is not clear whom they feared reprisals from: other gangsters, the magistrate's troops, or their own neighbors.

Wang San was long remembered by the people of T'an-ch'eng. Though his death from his wounds showed that he was not a heavenly spirit as some had believed, nevertheless people could not forget the extent of his operations, the size of his gang, or that final act of astonishing bravado: when he himself was the killer, coming in person to the court and standing guarantor for the man who had been falsely accused in his stead.

The Wangs had confessed to one of the crimes considered most serious in the *Legal Code,* "killing three persons in one family." The clause ran: "All those who kill, whether with premeditation, deliberately, in the course of burning their house, or while committing a robbery, three persons from the same family (none of whom were guilty of capital crimes), or who dismember another person, shall be executed by the lingering death; their property shall be made over to the surviving family of the deceased; their wives and sons shall be banished in perpetuity to a distance of 2000 *li;* and the main accessories shall be beheaded." One might have supposed, therefore, that Li Tung-chen's widow and his four surviving children, after time for the legal complications to be settled, would have ended up rich with money that Wang San had accumulated over the years. But this was not the case. When Huang took an inventory of Wang San's house in Wu-chang village, he found to his surprise that there was nothing of value in any of the three buildings, just some simple furnishings; and in the extensive stables, though the dung was feet deep on the floor, there were no horses, just a few donkeys. One of Wang's tenants supplied the answer: Wang kept nothing of value in T'an-ch'eng, he just used the county as his base; he shipped everything of value to P'ei, across the Kiangsu provincial boundary, where it was guarded for him by his blood brother, a senior degree holder named Chu. There is no evidence that the magistrate ever began the administrative and legal proceedings that would have been necessary to relieve a degree holder in Kiangsu of his property for transfer to a farming family in Shantung.

Five

THE
WOMAN
WHO
RAN
AWAY

IN THE WRITTEN and collected memory of T'an-ch'eng as it was stored in the biographical sections of the *Local History,* the highest standards were demanded and claimed. This was even truer for women than for men, and the dissemination of these biographies of "Honorable and Virtuous Women" was one of the important ways that the local worthies—acting in full accord with the stated values of the government—sought to impose their views of correct female behavior. By this they meant, in general, the behavior of women toward their husbands, for of the fifty-six T'an-ch'eng women's biographies printed in the 1670s, only three were of unmarried women, and of these three two were betrothed and about to be married. The virtues fostered were those of chastity, courage, tenacity, and unquestioning acceptance of the prevailing hierarchy—unto death if necessary: fifteen of the listed women had committed suicide, and in thirteen of these suicides the motive was loyalty to a deceased husband or to avoid rape, which would shame both wife and husband. In contrast to the suicides for vengeance, or out of anger, which Huang Liu-hung had criticized so strongly, these suicides (if by childless women) were considered morally "correct," as they showed the depth of the woman's reverence for her husband. They were praised even if the husband himself was no longer in good standing in the community—as can be seen from the case of woman Kao. This woman visited her seriously ill husband in the T'an-ch'eng prison, where he was being held on a murder charge; while in the cell she tried to hang both herself and him with the cloths used to bind her feet. Foiled in her attempt by the jailers, and barred from any further visits to the prison, she went to the temple of the City God and addressed him thus: "I wish to die as my husband is dying. His misery is my misery. How can I live on alone? My will is fixed: rather than die with him at the end, I shall be the one to go first. Only the God understands my situation." And she hanged herself on the verandah of the temple. Such suicides were not restricted to members of elite families who had been educated in the neo-Confucian ideals of loyalty: one woman Liu, who killed herself after her husband's death from illness, was a carpenter's daughter, her husband a farm laborer; another was married to a small trader who traveled back and forth between the market towns of Li-chia-chuang and Lai-wu.

The insistence on the wife's loyalty to the husband was so strong that it applied even when the couple were betrothed rather than married. When another woman Liu's fiancé,

Chang Shou, died before the ceremonies were completed and her parents secretly arranged her betrothal to another man, she "cut her hair and disfigured her face" and vowed that she would always be loyal to the man who would have been her husband. She insisted on serving Chang's parents as if they were her in-laws, and lived out her life with them in vegetarian abstemiousness. Even more poignant is the biography of a girl only thirteen years old who was living with the family of her future husband, Liu, in the village of Wang-t'ien, north of the county city. Such an arrangement was common enough at the time—a young girl could get food and protection, while her future mother-in-law got an extra pair of hands to help in the house. But in 1651, before the official marriage had taken place, Liu was slandered for having illicit relations with his widowed sister-in-law; with some impetuous notion of clearing her good name and proving his own integrity, he castrated himself. Both his parents and the young girl's mother argued that the betrothal contract was now broken, since Liu was "no longer a whole person," and they arranged for a new engagement. But as the new husband was being summoned, the young girl, on the pretext that she had to wash her body before receiving him, barred the door, and hanged herself.

Such stories were held in living memories as well as in the written record, and plenty of people were alive in 1671 to tell the present generation of past sacrifices: woman Wang's father-in-law was in his seventies; the former district headman, Yü Shun, was over ninety; widow Fan was eighty-one, and her biography shows she had already borne her son by the time of the great famine of 1615—when "men sold their wives for a few tens of cash, or sold their sons for the price of a few steamed dumplings"—and was a widow by 1622, when the White Lotus rebels enticed so many from T'an-ch'eng to their fate. For most of these old survivors, as for the newer generations, the grimmest of the stories must have clustered about the Manchu sack of their city in 1643, and it was from these stories that some of the most exemplary cases could be drawn. At least nine of the women listed in the T'an-ch'eng biographies lost their husbands to the Manchus in that year, and descriptions were kept of how four other upright women met their ends: Woman Hsieh and woman T'ien, who had married two brothers and shared the same home, hanged themselves from the same beam with their sashes as the troops approached; one was twenty-four, the other twenty. Woman Ho, who had been left a widow by her husband's death five years before, was caught by soldiers as she tried to flee with her six-year-old daughter; when she resisted them they struck her with their swords, but she broke away and flung herself into a well, holding her daughter in her arms. The next day neighbors heard the little girl crying, and they rescued her, but woman Ho was dead. As the troops looted the outer rooms of her home, woman Ch'en waited with her eight-year-old son in the main hall of her private apartment. Her husband was away, somewhere in the city, trying with the help of his brother to carry their mother to safety. The woman Ch'en and her son were both crying. Soldiers entered the room and dragged her outside, across the courtyard. She struggled, shouting and swearing at them. She was still cursing when they pulled her through the main gateway into the street, so they killed her.

Others survived in T'an-ch'eng, but narrowly. Woman Hsü was captured by the troops and wounded, but she managed to escape with her six-year-old son. Woman Yang was seven months pregnant when the soldiers killed her husband and her mother-in-law. She proceeded publicly with the funeral rites for them, and the soldiers let her be. (Two months later, when the armies had departed, she bore a son.) Woman Kao jumped from the city wall holding her five-year-old son after the troops had killed her husband and the older children. She ran to the east, and would have drowned while trying to cross the Shu River, but she was rescued by local villagers who sheltered her and the boy.

P'u Sung-ling paid his own homage to such women's courage in a brief story called "Chang's Wife":

In the year 1674, when the Three Feudatories had risen in rebellion, the expeditionary troops being sent south were bivouacked with their horses in the area of Yen; not a dog or chicken was left, the hearths were empty, women and girls all suffered their outrages.

At this season there had been heavy rains, and the fields were covered in water, like lakes; the people had nowhere to hide, so they climbed over the walls and went into the fields of standing kaoliang. Knowing this, the troops stripped off their clothes and rode naked on their horses after them, tracking them down in the water and raping them. Few escaped.

Only the wife of a certain Chang did not lie low but stayed quite openly in her own home. At night, with her husband, she dug a deep pit in her kitchen and filled it with dried reeds; she screened over the top and laid matting upon it so that it looked like a bed. And then she went on with her cooking by the stove.

When the troops came to the village she went out of the door of the house, as if offering herself. Two Mongol soldiers seized her and prepared to rape her, but she said to them, "How can I do such a thing in the presence of others?" One of them chuckled, jabbered to the other, and went away. The woman went into the house with the other and pointed at the bed, to get him to climb up first. The screening broke, and the soldier tumbled in. The woman took the matting and again placed it on the screen over the hole; then she stood by it, to lure the other when he came. He returned after a short while and heard the shouting from within the pit, though he couldn't tell where it was; the woman beckoned to him with her hand and her smile, saying, "Over here." The soldier climbed onto the matting and also fell in. The woman threw more brushwood on top of them and set the whole pile on fire. The flames blazed up, and the house itself caught fire. The woman called out for help. When the fire was extinguished, there was a strong smell of roasted flesh; people asked her what it was, and the woman replied, "I had two pigs, and feared they would be taken from me by the troops. So I hid them in that pit."

"An excellent use of strategies," added P'u Sung-ling, in one of the brief comments he liked to append to his own stories, "without losing one's body to the voracious soldiers. A worthy woman indeed. Intelligent and also fit to be numbered among the 'loyal and virtuous'!"

This story was apparently considered too outspoken by P'u Sung-ling's Ch'ing-dynasty editors, and they cut it from the printed collection of his stories. Perhaps to contemporaries these "Mongols" were transparently Manchu, and the story verged, therefore, on the treasonous. But in many other stories P'u Sung-ling confronted his women not with outside ravagers but with other, more complex social challenges:

A scholar named Tsung Hsiang-jo, on an autumn day, went out to inspect his fields, and saw, at a spot where the ripe grain grew thickly, signs of violent motion. Puzzled, he walked along the path between the fields to take a look, and found a man and woman coupling. Laughing, he started to turn back, but the man, embarrassed, fastened his belt and scurried away.

The woman also stood up. Looking her over closely, the scholar saw that she was very lovely; attracted to her, he would have liked to make love to her himself, but he felt ashamed to do so out in the country dirt. Coming close to her, he brushed off the soil, and asked, "Do you like these illicit assignations in the country-side?" The woman smiled, but did not answer.

Tsung drew her body to him and opened her dress; her flesh

was glossy as lard, and he ran his hands up and down over her several times. The woman smiled and said, "You're a rotten scholar. You just do whatever you feel like doing. Why do you feel me over in this crazy way?" He asked her name, and she replied, "Like the wind in spring we pass by once, and then go our ways in opposite directions; why take the trouble to find out more about me? Do you want to make a note of my name so you can erect a tablet to my chastity?"

Said Tsung: "This coupling out in the wet grass of the country-side is something for swineherds from mountain villages; it's not my way. If someone as beautiful as you wants to have affairs, she should value herself more highly. Why debase yourself like this?" The woman seemed to agree completely with his words, so Tsung said to her, "My poor lodging is not far from here. I pray you come by and spend some time with me."

The woman succumbed to this approach, and the same night, in the comfort of his home, the two made love.

Local society offered P'u Sung-ling endless sources of in-spiration, since he was intrigued by the entire gamut of prob-lems that lurked within sensual relationships: the cash nexus, first of all, and from various of his stories one can compile a list of his rather mocking estimate of comparative female costs: though one night with the finest courtesan might cost a man fifteen taels, the permanent possession of such a beauty be had for a thousand, two hundred buy a young singing girl, and one hundred a decent-looking concubine, one would need only ten taels to obtain an ugly bad-tempered wife who had been the maid of a local gentry family, and three taels would buy a plain wife for a peasant widower (one tael of the three went to the scribe for drawing up the contract, a few coppers to the go-between, and a little over one tael to the bride's family). P'u was similarly interested in the details behind different kinds of divorces, by vengeance in the family setting, by betrayal and frustration, by homosexual literati, by the special problems of plain women. As he put it in the epilogue to one of his stories, "The Country of the Savages," "These savages are said to be rare, but if you think about it they are not so rare—in the beds of every household there is some savage present." He was interested in strong women who could have their babies and go right on working, in women who could bring up illegitimate children, in women who determined not to marry at all but to follow the way of the Immortal Ho Hsien-ku in a life of virginity—Ho Hsien-ku was a spirit who had appeared in the temple of that other female immortal, Ma Ku, herself, by some accounts, a native of T'an-ch'eng. He was also amused if the man could keep his wit in face of a woman's reluctance:

"As the man moved to embrace her, the woman said, 'Take your hands off me for a moment. There are two ways now before us, and I ask you to choose one of them.' He asked her what she meant, and she replied, 'If we have a friendship in which we play *wei-ch'i* and drink together, then we will be able to spend thirty years in each other's company; but if we indulge in the pleasures of the bedchamber, we can be together only six years. Which do you choose?' And the man replied, 'Let's talk it over again in six years' time.' "

Yet P'u Sung-ling was delighted too by the naïveté of the scholar so deep in his books that he had never realized there was such a thing as sex until, initiated by a beautiful woman, he rushed out to tell all the neighbors. And he wrote his own variant on the traditional theme of "Mu-lan"—the martial young woman who dresses up as a man and goes to fight the frontier battles with the army in her father's stead—in his story of "Woman Yen." Well educated and married to a silly and pretentious scholar who is constantly failing the examinations, she lashes out at him, "You are not a real man, although you wear the cap of one. If you would let me change to a man's hair style and hat, I could pass those exams as easily as I pluck a mustard plant from the ground." The man is furious at hearing these words, his eyes flash, and he answers angrily, "You women have never been in the examination halls and think that attaining official rank and becoming a powerful personage is as easy as it is for you in the kitchen to draw water from the well and boil the rice." But finally he has the grace to let her try, and, her big man's shoes stuffed with cotton wadding to keep them on her tiny feet, she passes the examinations triumphantly and becomes a senior official.

P'u was also willing, despite withdrawals into irony or fantasy, to note realistically how sexual deference could kill the weaker party:

Nan San-fu came from one of the renowned families of Chinyang. He had a country retreat about ten *li* away from his home, and one day as he was riding there he was caught in a sudden rain storm; seeing, in the village through which he was passing, a peasant's house that looked moderately spacious, he resolved to shelter there. Since the neighboring villagers all looked up to Nan, the owner of the house hurried out to greet him with the greatest deference. The room Nan entered was tiny; after he sat down there, the owner took up a broom to sweep the floor and scattered water to lay the dust. The host prepared Nan a drink of tea mixed with honey, and only when Nan insisted did he even dare to sit down himself.

Nan asked him his name, and he answered, "T'ing-chang, surnamed Tou." After a short while Tou offered his guest some wine, and then some chicken, all of it served most respectfully. A girl, already grown up, served the food and kept hovering just outside the door, so that Nan caught glimpses of her body; she was fifteen or sixteen, and so demure and pretty that Nan felt his heart pounding. The rain stopped and he returned home, but he could not rid himself of thoughts of her.

The day after that he took some food and some cloth over to Tou's house, to thank him and to further his cause; from then on, whenever he passed by their house, he would bring some food or wine, and enjoy a drink with Tou. The girl gradually grew acquainted with him and no longer bothered to follow custom and keep out of the way. She would not hesitate to come into his presence, and if Nan stared at her she would lower her head, smiling slightly.

Nan was ever more enchanted by her; he could not let three days pass without going to see her—until one day Tou happened to be out. Nan sat and waited a long time for Tou to return, until finally the girl came out to greet the guest. Nan tugged her to him by the arm and tried to seduce her, but she, flushed and angry, pushed him away, saying, "I may be poor, but if you want me as a wife, why try and overwhelm me with your wealth and arrogance?" Nan, whose own wife had recently died, bowed before the girl and said, "If you have pity on me and care for me, I will take no other to wife." The girl asked him to swear to it, and after Nan had pointed to heaven and vowed his eternal faithfulness, she gave herself to him.

From then on, whenever Tou was out of the house, the two of them made love. The girl kept urging Nan, saying, "We cannot keep this relationship secret for long; when you agree to marry me my parents will be deeply honored and make no trouble at all. You must find a way to do it soon!" Nan agreed to this but kept wondering whether he ought to unite himself with the daughter of a peasant, and so put things off with one excuse or another. Then it happened that a marriage broker offered him a wife from a fine family—Nan at first couldn't make up his mind, but when he heard that the potential bride was also both beautiful and rich, he decided to marry her.

The girl Tou was now pregnant, and urged Nan all the more to marry her, but he severed the relationship and stopped coming to see her; her time came and she gave birth to a son. Her father was furious and hit her until she confessed everything; only when she said Nan had promised to marry her, Tou desisted and sent off an intermediary to contact Nan. Nan at once denied it. So Tou put the baby out of the house and beat his daughter all the harder. Secretly she sent the wife of a neighbor to tell Nan about her anguish, but Nan made no response.

That night the girl ran away; she found her baby outside, still living, and clasping it to her, she hastened to Nan. She beat on his door, and called out to the gatekeeper, "If I can have just one word with your master, I will be saved from death; even if he spares no thought for me, does that mean that he has none for his child?" The gatekeeper reported these words to Nan, but Nan forbade him to let her enter—and the girl, leaning on the gate, wept bitterly. At around three in the morning the sound ceased; and when it grew light they saw her, seated, dead, with the baby in her arms.

P'u Sung-ling was not sentimental about marriage, despite the contentment of his own. He knew that for many women marriage could prove to be a joyless trap; sometimes he offered such women a vision of escape, as in the bleak story "Yün Ts'ui-hsien":

L iang Yu-ts'ai grew up in Shansi but moved later to Shantung, where he made his living as a peddler. He had no wife, no children, and no landed property.

When the local villagers climbed Mount T'ai, he used to accompany them; in the fourth month all the people going to offer incense on Mount T'ai moved along like a stream, together with Buddhist monks and nuns who brought along groups of men by the tens or hundreds, and all these people knelt together in great confusion at the foot of the holy altars while they watched their sticks of incense burn down. This was the ceremony called "kneeling to offer incense."

Among the crowd Ts'ai saw a girl of seventeen or eighteen who was very beautiful and attracted him strongly. Pretending to be one of the people who had come to burn incense, he moved over and knelt down next to the girl; then, acting as though he had a pain in his knees and did not have the strength to stend up, he pressed down on the ground with his hands and pressed against her foot at the same time. She turned her head, apparently angry, and moved away from him on her knees. Ts'ai, still on his knees, followed her and after a moment pressed her foot again. Understanding what his intentions were, the girl stood up and without kneeling down again walked out of the door and left. Ts'ai also got up and went out to follow her, but couldn't see which way she had gone. He gave up hope of finding her and had started to return home, dejectedly, when on the road he saw the girl again, walking along with an old woman who seemed to be her mother. Ts'ai hurried up behind them as they were strolling along talking, and heard the old woman say, "You have paid your homage to the Goddess of Childbirth, which was a good act indeed. Since you have no younger brothers or sisters dependent on you, if only the Goddess will give you this added protection in the underworld, and in this world help you to find a good husband who is filial and equitable, then it would not matter that he was not from a fine family or a wealthy home."

Ts'ai was delighted at hearing this, and gradually drawing level with them he began to question the old lady. She told him that she was from the Yün family, that the girl—whose given name was Ts'ui-hsien—was her own daughter and that their house was forty *li* away in the western hills.

"The mountain road is hard," said Ts'ai. "With your slow tread, and your daughter's dainty steps, how will you be able to get back there?"

"It is already late, and I shall stay over at my brother's house," the old lady replied.

Said Ts'ai: "Just now you were saying that your son-in-law

might be poor or of lowly birth; I am not married. Might I prove satisfactory to you?"

The old woman asked the girl her opinion, but she would not answer. Finally, after the woman had asked her several times, the girl replied, "This fellow is not rich; he is also lecherous, frivolous, and easily swayed. I would not want to be the wife of such a dissolute man."

Hearing this, Ts'ai swore by the sun that he was absolutely sincere. The old woman was pleased, and finally agreed to his proposal; but the girl was not happy, responding only by an angry look, for which her mother slapped and scolded her.

Ts'ai was diligent in his attentions; he put his hand into his purse and hired the services of two mountain chairs and porters for the woman and the girl, while he walked along on foot behind them, as if he were their servant. Whenever they came to a dangerous spot on the mountain track, he would call out to the porters not to stumble and not to shake the chairs, as if he were extremely solicitous. They arrived thus at the village, and Ts'ai was invited with them into the house of the girl's uncle. The uncle, who came out to greet them, was an old man, and his wife, who also came out, was old as well. The old lady Yün referred to them as "elder brother" and "sister-in-law," and told them, "Ts'ai is now my son-in-law. Since this is an auspicious day, there is no need to wait for another; the marriage can be held this evening."

Ts'ui-hsien's uncle was delighted, and brought out wine and food for Ts'ai. After a short while Ts'ui-hsien appeared in special attire; the bed was all prepared, and they retired for the night. Ts'ui-hsien said to her husband, "I know that you have not been a moral person; compelled by my mother's command I have been forced to go along with you. But if you behave in a decent human fashion, it should not be too painful for us to live together." Ts'ai most respectfully took note of these words.

Having risen early the next morning, the mother said to Ts'ai, "It would be best for you to go on ahead; my daughter and I will come on later." So Ts'ai went back and tidied up his house; later the old lady escorted her daughter there. When they looked around inside they saw that it was completely bare of furniture, and the old lady said, "How can you survive, living in such a fashion? Let me hurry back home, and help alleviate this misery a little." She departed, and the next day a group of men and women arrived, bringing clothing, food, and various useful objects; they filled the house with them and left without even taking a meal. Just one maid was left behind to be with the couple.

From this time on Ts'ai sat about, warmly clothed and well fed. Every day he invited the wastrels of the village to drink with him and to gamble; and he began to steal Ts'ui-hsien's hair ornaments and earrings in order to get more gambling money. When she protested he ignored her; and when she could stand it no more she began to keep strict watch over her jewelry boxes, as though she were defending them against robbers.

One day a group of his gambling friends knocked at the door to visit Ts'ai and happened to catch a glimpse of Ts'ui-hsien. They were completely dumbfounded and said to Ts'ai in jest, "You are a very rich man; why do you keep complaining about your poverty?" Ts'ai asked what they meant, and one of the men answered, "We just got a look at your wife, she's indeed as lovely as a fairy. She married you, but she comes from quite a different social level; if you sold her off to be someone's concubine you could get a hundred taels for her; if you sold her to be a prostitute you could get a thousand. With a thousand taels in the house, what would stop you drinking and gambling as much as you choose?" Ts'ai didn't reply directly, but in his heart he agreed with them.

Thereafter, when Ts'ai was in his wife's presence, he would sometimes suddenly sigh, at other times complain that his poverty was unbearable. If she paid no attention to him Ts'ai would start to bang his fists on the table, throw the knives and chopsticks around, curse at the maidservant, and keep on with this sort of behavior. One night Ts'ui-hsien bought some wine, which she drank with her husband. Suddenly she said, "You are unhappy every day because of your poverty; I cannot prevent these deprivations either; I share your unhappiness. How can I help being ashamed? I have no valuable possessions, nothing except this one maidservant. If we sold her, you could take the money and start some kind of business."

But Ts'ai shook his head, saying, "What value does she have?"

They drank for a little longer, and Ts'ui-hsien said, "Why could you and I not have been happy together? But now I have no strength left. It seems to me that our poverty has reached such a level that we could be together until death without ever being able to do more than share a lifetime of miseries, with no chance that our fortunes would improve. It would be better if you sold me to some wealthy household; both of us would profit, and you would get much more than if you sold the maidservant."

Ts'ai, pretending to be astonished, asked, "How could I ever go that far?" But since Ts'ui-hsien continued to talk about it, and her face showed her seriousness, Ts'ai was happy and said, "We'll think it over again later."

So Ts'ai made arrangements with the eunuch of a powerful local family to sell her and have her registered in the category of courtesans; the eunuch came in person to visit Ts'ai, and when he saw Ts'ui-hsien he was greatly taken with her. Fearing that something might arise to prevent the deal, he immediately drew up a bond for eight hundred taels, and so the matter was concluded.

"My mother has been constantly worried about the poverty of her son-in-law's household," said Ts'ui-hsien to her husband. "Now that the bonds between us have been severed, I would like to pay her a visit and take my leave. Besides, how can I not tell my mother that you and I have separated?" Ts'ai was worried that her mother might try to raise some obstacles, but the girl reassured him: "I am perfectly contented, and can guarantee she won't interfere."

Ts'ai agreed to go. The night was half over when they reached her mother's house; banging on the outer door, they passed into the court, and Ts'ai saw a magnificent house of several stories, in which maids and men servants moved back and forth in continual bustle. Now during all the time that Ts'ai had lived with Ts'ui-hsien, whenever he had asked to visit her mother, his wife had always prevented it, so that though he had been her son-in-law for over a year, he had never once visited her home. He was astonished at the magnificence of the house and feared that Ts'ui-hsien would never consent to becoming a concubine or singing girl. Ts'ui-hsien led Ts'ai to the upper floor; surprised, the old lady asked the couple why they had come. Ts'ui-hsien replied bitterly, "I said from the first that this man was untrustworthy, and now I have been proven right." And taking two bars of gold out from inside her dress, she placed them on the table, saying, "Luckily they were not stolen by this worthless fellow, so now I can return them to my mother." The mother was surprised and asked what had happened. "This fellow tried to sell me; there is nothing for me to do with this gold I had stored away."

Then pointing at Ts'ai, Ts'ui-hsien cursed him: "You vicious rat! You used to carry loads on a pole across your back, your face was streaked with dust like a demon's. When you first approached me I was suffocated by the rank smell of your sweat; the filth of your skin rotted the bed; on your hands and feet were sores an inch across which nauseated me the whole night through. After I married you and went to your house, you sat at your ease and ate your food, but your devil's nature finally appeared. In front of my own mother, how dare I lie about such things?"

Ts'ai hung his head and did not even dare let his breath out. Ts'ui-hsien continued: "I know that I am not especially beautiful and might not be able to satisfy some great personage, but I would have thought I would make a good enough match for someone of your type! In what was I lacking that you should show me no trace of affection? Had I chosen to I could have built us a lofty home, and bought us luxuriant fields; but I could see you were the kind who cheats those closest to him, and whines like a beggar. You would not be a fit companion for my old age!"

As Ts'ui-hsien was speaking, the servant girls and the old women rolled up their sleeves to the elbows and formed a circle around Ts'ai; hearing the charges she was making about him, they all began to spit at him and curse him, and said to Ts'ui-hsien, "He should be killed. What's the point of going on with all this talking?" Ts'ai was terrified; he fell to the ground and admitted that he had done wrong but that he was now truly penitent.

Ts'ui-hsien cried out even more angrily: "It is bad enough that you wanted to sell your own wife, yet that was not enough for you; how could you dare to sell the woman who had shared your bed to be a common prostitute?" Before she had finished speaking, the whole group, with eyes glaring wide, jabbed into Ts'ai's sides and legs with sharp hairpins, with scissors, with knives. Ts'ai screamed out, and begged for his life, and Ts'ui-hsien told the servants to stop, saying, "You can let him go for now. Although the fellow has been so unworthy, I cannot bear to see him trembling with fear in this way." And she led them all downstairs.

Ts'ai sat there a long time, listening, until the voices had all died away, hoping that he might be able to make his escape. Suddenly, looking up, he saw the stars shining, and in the east signs of dawn. The country was deserted, enclosed by woods. Gradually the last lights flickered out, there was no house at all, and Ts'ai found he was sitting on the edge of a precipice. Looking down, he could see the steep ravine but not the bottom of its depths; he was terrified with the fear of falling; he moved his body slightly and heard a thump, and he and the rock on which he was sitting slid down over the edge. Halfway down the cliff there was a dead tree leaning out at an angle, which stopped Ts'ai falling to the bottom—it supported his shoulders, though he could not grasp it with his hands or feet; looking down, he could see only the void; there was no way of guessing how deep it might be. He did not dare turn around or bend, he yelled out in his terror, his whole body swelled up, and eyes, ears, nose, tongue, every part of his body lost its strength.

Slowly the sun rose in the sky, and at last a woodcutter came by and saw Ts'ai. The woodcutter went off to fetch a rope, which he lowered down, and pulled Ts'ai back up the precipice; and since Ts'ai was gasping for breath and seemed near death, the woodcutter carried him back to his home. The door of Ts'ai's house swung open, and inside it was as desolate as a ruined temple: the beds, the chests, the household objects all were gone, and nothing remained but the torn bedding and a broken table, the original possessions that he had had before his marriage. Ts'ai lay down, distracted; and each day, when he was hungry, he begged for food from the neighbors. By and by his swollen body started to fester; his former friends in the village despised what he had done; they all began to spit on him and to spurn him. Ts'ai had no idea what to do; he sold his house, moved into a shack, and would go out to beg along the roadside.

He always carried a knife with him, and if someone urged him to exchange the knife for some food, Ts'ai would refuse, saying, "I live in a wild place and must protect myself from tigers and wolves. I use this to guard myself."

Some time later he happened to run into one of the men who had urged him to sell his wife. Ts'ai walked up to him and began a lamentation; then suddenly pulling out the knife, he stabbed and killed the man. When the official investigating the case heard all the circumstances he could not bear to give Ts'ai a cruel punishment, and so had him confined in jail. Ts'ai died there, in prison, from cold and hunger.

But what of the women of T'an-ch'eng with no recourse to magic or to money? What of the woman called Wang who married a man called Jen?

We do not know exactly when they married, though it

must have been some time in the late 1660s, nor do we know their personal names. We do not even know how Jen could afford a wife, since there were many fewer women than men available in T'an-ch'eng due to a combination of factors: female infanticide, the lower levels of food supplied to girls, the presence always of several women in the homes of wealthier men. Jen might not have had to pay any cash, or even furnish the customary presents to get woman Wang as his wife, for she seems to have been an orphan—or at least to have had no surviving relatives living nearby—and since Jen's own father was a widower of seventy, she might have been brought in as a young girl to help with the household chores and married to Jen when she was old enough, as was often done with young girls in the country.

What we do know about the couple is this: By early 1671 they were married and living in a small village outside the market town of Kuei-ch'ang, eight miles southwest of T'an-ch'eng city. They were poor, and Jen made his living as a hired laborer on other people's land. They had a one-room house that contained a cooking pot, a lamp, a woven sleeping mat, and a straw mattress. We know too that for six months after the marriage woman Wang had lived with her husband and her seventy-year-old father-in-law, but that the old man finally moved to another house a mile away because he got on so badly with her. And we know that woman Wang was left alone much of the day; that she had bound feet; that she had no children, though there was a little girl living in a house next door who called her "Auntie"; that her house fronted onto a small wood; and that at some time, for some reason, as the year 1671 advanced, she ran away.

She ran away with another man, though we do not know his name, nor where the two of them intended to go. We can see from the map that they had three initial choices: they could move southwest and cross the border into P'ei; they could walk eight miles northeast to the county city of T'an-ch'eng and from there follow the post road, either south to Hung-hua fou and into Kiangsu, or north to I-chou and on into central Shantung; or they could walk eight miles northwest to Ma-t'ou, and from Ma-t'ou head west on the road that led to Chang-ch'eng market and on into T'eng and Tsou counties. Whichever route they chose, unless they could afford carriers or a cart, they would have to move slowly on account of woman Wang's bound feet.

P'ei would not have been a bad choice if they wanted to avoid pursuit. The way there was hilly, but the countryside had for years supported bandits and fugitives who had played the change of provincial jurisdiction to their advantage. One could even travel part of the way by light boat down the River I in summer and autumn when the water level was high and the authorities in P'ei were unlikely to worry about one more fugitive couple. P'ei had been struck by catastrophes as serious as those in T'an-ch'eng—famine, locusts, and war, cycles of drought and flood. P'ei had also suffered from the earthquake of 1668, though less than T'an-ch'eng, but since P'ei was on the Yellow River, flood was a potential catastrophe, which it never was in T'an-ch'eng, with its smaller tributary rivers; and a month after the earthquake high winds and swollen water levels tearing at the banks had broken the land, and much of the city of P'ei fell beneath the waves. Only one or two hundred families escaped, and in the period when T'an-ch'eng slowly began to recover, in P'ei the population dropped by another third.

T'an-ch'eng city was in some ways an obvious goal, but the disadvantages were also obvious. As the site of the magistrate's yamen and the center of county administration, security was tighter than anywhere else. Regulations that remained only on paper elsewhere in the county were enforced here: there were regular patrols outside the city and checkpoints on the roads nearby. Travelers could be stopped for questioning and made to explain their reasons for wanting to enter the city, even refused entrance unless they had relatives living there. The inns were notorious for their dishonesty: many were run by dishonest owners who lured the unwary with displays of cheap food and wine; but once the country folk had registered, the bills began to climb, and outsiders and hangers-on charged items on their accounts. If the guests tried to move to other lodgings they found it impossible, since the innkeepers hired goons to threaten the owners of other places to which they might go. Even if the innkeepers were honest, those within the city walls were expected to keep a daily register of all travelers who lodged there, whether individuals or groups; they also had to note their origins and destinations, the goods they might have for sale, their mules or carts, their weapons if they had them. Armed horsemen without luggage or goods were forbidden to hire grooms or to stay in town overnight. Even lone foot travelers, whether armed or not, could be moved on if they had no baggage and no one in the city to vouch for them. No walking around in the city was permitted after nightfall, though during the hottest summer months the people whose homes had no halls or courtyards were allowed to have their doors ajar and sit on the stoops to enjoy the evening coolness. But the wooden gates that led from the alleys out to the main streets were closed and guarded at nightfall, and only those seeking emergency help from a doctor or midwife were allowed to pass—and then only if they had a regulation "night travel permit," duly authenticated, and if their residence and identity had been checked.

Certainly Ma-t'ou market would seem a more attractive choice for a couple seeking to hide out. Despite its size it had few garrison troops and no senior officials in residence. It had been attacked twice by bandits, in 1641 and 1648, but regained prosperity rapidly—as we can tell by a number of indices. Its major market days on the third and eighth day of every ten-day cycle, and the lesser market days on the fifth and tenth, dictated the market cycle of the surrounding areas. It was the only town with significant trade being moved by both road and water, trade that was worth taxing. It had a sizable urban working population, strong trade guilds, more temples than the other towns, more gardens, larger religious festivals. It was the only town in the county that supported a family of well-known physicians.

The couple needed somewhere to hide, for by the mere act of running away from her husband, woman Wang had become a criminal in the eyes of the law. Only if a wife was severely hurt or mutilated by her husband, or if she was forced by him to commit sexual acts with others, was she free to leave him. An example of a husband who by his actions put himself beyond the pale of the married relationship was furnished in Ning-yang, northwest of T'an-ch'eng (and also in Yen prefecture), in a case that was cited by jurists in the K'ang-hsi reign: a husband who sold his wife off as a prostitute and subsequently, having been forced by the magistrate to take her back, connived at her adultery with their lodging-house keeper, was considered to have "severed the bonds of marriage." But barring acts of this nature by the husband, the woman who ran away was classified as a fugitive and subject to a punishment of one hundred blows. All those who helped her or sheltered her—unless they could prove total ignorance of her fugitive status—could be subject to punishment in the same way as those who harbored fugitives or the wives and daughters of military deserters.

The act of adultery, furthermore, made both woman Wang and her paramour liable to serious punishment. The *Legal Code* stipulated that those having illegal intercourse by mutual consent were to be punished with eighty blows; if the woman was married, with ninety blows; if they intrigued to meet away from the woman's house, with one hundred blows, whether the woman was married or not. The man and the woman who had illegal intercourse, by mutual consent or after intriguing to meet away from the woman's house, received identical punishment. If the woman gave birth to a child after the illegal intercourse, the natural father met the expenses of raising it. The husband could sell off his adulterous wife or keep her, as he chose; but if he sold her in marriage to the adulterer, then both the husband and the adulterer were punished with eighty blows, the woman had to be divorced and returned to her family, and the price originally paid for her was forfeited to the government.

The punishment could be more serious than this, however, since the husband was considered justified in killing either his wife or the adulterer or both if he caught them in the act and slew them while in his initial rage. As in the case of killing to revenge a parent, the husband had to act swiftly, and in 1646 a rider had been added to the law, presumably to prevent vendettas or extended pursuit in the desire for revenge, stating that the husband was not justified in killing either of the adulterers if they merely were dallying before committing the sexual act, or if they had committed adultery but surrendered to him on their own, or "if he caught them in a place other than that where the adultery was committed." Thus by leaving Jen's house without being caught, woman Wang and her lover became legally more secure.

Not that life on the road can have been particularly secure, even if it was lively. The list of people technically under the supervision of the "Inspector of Humble Professions"—whose office like so much else in T'an-ch'eng had been burned down in the 1640s and not yet rebuilt—included such wandering specialists as fortunetellers, diviners, physiognomists and graphologists, jugglers, conjurers, actors, jesters and street wrestlers, storytellers and itinerant Buddhist and Taoist priests, woman dentists and midwives, the chiefs of the beggar groups, pipers, drummers, flute players, firecracker makers, tea sellers, and chair bearers. Huang Liu-hung's own reports often mentioned grooms, yamen runners, couriers and clerks from the post stations, the staffs of the state-managed hostels, and crowds of peddlers so poor and so numerous—their stalls under matting sheds in rows on the streets—that Huang gave up all attempts to tax them. Besides these there were refugees, fugitives from justice, and army deserters. Despite the regulations, such people could often find work, since farmers valued them as a source of cheap labor and asked no questions, while restaurant and lodging-house keepers would give them food and shelter if they could pay; making a living was more important than following the exact letter of the registration laws.

Indeed, there seems to have been a virtual fugitive subculture with its own rules and its own exploitations, inevitably involving the law-abiding civilian population because of the strict laws against harboring fugitives and the rigors of mutual responsibility under the *pao-chia* registration system. We see something of the fugitives' world from a case reported in T'an-ch'eng where a fugitive was used to harass an enemy in a private commercial feud. The police clerk Wei accused the innkeeper Shih Wen-yü of hiring a fugitive for three hundred cash a month to work at his inn on the very steps of the T'an-ch'eng magistrate's yamen. Wei attempted to have Shih imprisoned on this charge; investigation showed, however, that the story was a trumped-up one (though the fugitive was real enough), fabricated by Wei so that he would not have to pay for the hundred or more cups of wine he had drunk on credit in Shih's inn over the previous year. Wei had blackmailed the fugitive into making the false charge. In such cases it was not so much that the fugitive's testimony had to be believed, but rather that his presence had to be disproved, which was not always easy; on this occasion Shih was luckily proved innocent, since the magistrate held an informal police line-up at which the fugitive could not distinguish Shih from a neighboring bean-curd seller. Other cases show that soldiers also harassed the innocent through a fairly subtle confidence game: Soldier A, pretending to be a fugitive, would go into a moored boat or some isolated village; other soldiers would then come and "arrest" him, pretending to be police runners, harassing the locals for harboring a fugitive, and robbing them as they left. Or perhaps they would briefly build up an identity in some village as hired hands and then, when all were drunk together one evening, cut themselves up, tear their own clothes, and claim they had been "robbed" in order to get hush money from the local villagers; if suspicions began to be aroused, one of their friends would come claiming to be a superior officer from the fugitive unit, and would reclaim them. At times it might be the ferrymen themselves running the rackets and claiming far more than the stipulated rate of one copper coin a person and two coppers per mule: demanding extra money in rain or snow or late at night, extra to allow a coffin on their boat, or holding passengers to ransom when out in the middle of the stream. While ashore the ferry guard might levy his own "taxes" and confiscate the goods of those who refused to pay, or fondle the women and make them pay to be released.

If it was hard for the two of them on the run, it must have been a nightmare for woman Wang after her lover abandoned her a short time later and left her alone on the road. The society of T'an-ch'eng did not supply many jobs for women, even if they were regarded as reputable: a few became midwives or diviners; some who were trusted and well known locally served as marriage go-betweens and as guarantors who would take responsibility for the women prisoners in the local jail. A few jobs were available in the orphanages and the homes for the totally indigent and the old, where women were employed as nurses, as children's companions, or as watchmen, as well as houseworkers to clean up and do laundry. For such work they would get their keep and an allowance of three hundred copper cash a month, or else a flat wage of six taels a year—roughly equivalent to the wages of men in the poorer positions in the local yamen. Those women who had the resources for a loom could spin and sell the product, but that was usually work done in one's own home, and woman Wang now had no home. If they were at the right place at the right time, they might get a job as a maid in one of the larger households. There was a slight chance of becoming a worker in a Taoist or Buddhist convent. Otherwise the main employment must have been in the gambling houses, teahouses, and brothels of T'an-ch'eng, of Ma-t'ou market, of Hung-hua post station, even—according to Huang Liu-hung—in quite isolated rural villages, where local gentry set up brothels just as in the urban centers, giving protection to the women and taking a percentage of their money in return.

Woman Wang chose none of these alternatives, nor did she continue her flight alone. What she did was head back to her original home in Kuei-ch'ang; but when she got near the house she was too frightened to confront her husband Jen.

Near her village stood a Taoist temple to the Three Forces—the heavens, the waters, and the earth—forces that could bring happiness (heaven), remission of sins (water), and protection from evil (earth). Here she was given shelter by the sole resident of the temple, a Taoist priest; and here a former neighbor of hers, Kao, came to offer incense one day in November 1671 and caught a glimpse of her in one of the side rooms of the temple.

"You are in charge of a temple to the gods," he shouted to the priest. "What do you mean by keeping women in here?"

"She's the wife of a man called Jen in the village," the priest replied. "I heard that she ran off with someone, and Jen went out looking for her to get her back. But she didn't dare return home and took shelter here. Because she is one of our villagers, it would not have been good to just send her away."

While they were still talking about her, Jen himself came into the temple, having learned that woman Wang had returned and was hiding there. "A fine kind of priest you are," he shouted angrily. "My wife hides out in your temple and you don't even tell me about it."

"She's the wife from your house," countered Kao. "Why should she end up at the temple? You don't even know that, and now you want the priest to explain it to you?"

Even angrier, Jen shouted, "Oh, so in that case it must be you who hid her out here in the temple," and at this insult Kao hit him twice in the face. Jen swore at him and left, leaving his wife where she was.

This sudden outburst of rage between the two men may have been because of some long pent-up grievance—they were neighbors, Kao was comparatively well off, with a covered porch to his house and a wife named Ts'ao whom Jen also seems to have disliked. But Kao should not have hit Jen, however severe the insult; the *Legal Code* was strict about this and drew distinctions about fights of this kind with such minute attention to detail that they were clearly regarded as a major problem. Any person striking another with a hand or foot was to be punished with twenty blows if he caused no wound, with thirty blows if he caused a wound; any person striking another with an object of any kind would receive thirty blows if no wound was caused, forty if there was a wound—a wound being defined by discoloration or swelling in the place struck, as well as by bleeding. Tearing out more than one inch of hair was punished with fifty blows, striking another so as to cause internal bleeding with eighty blows; eighty blows too for throwing ordure at the head of another, and a hundred blows for stuffing ordure into his mouth or nose, for breaking a tooth or bone, or injuring the eyes. (In cases where permanent injury was caused, the offender forfeited half his property to pay the support of the injured party.)

Jen now had a real grievance against Kao, one that would fester for months, but he did not press any charges against him—presumably the situation was too humiliating to air any more publicly. Yet the incident had been awkward enough for both Kao and the priest, and they decided it would be wiser to make woman Wang leave the temple, though they hesitated to send her back to her husband right away. Instead they took her to her father-in-law and explained what had taken place. The father-in-law gave the two men tea. "There's nothing at all that I can do about this bitch," said he, and called a fellow to take woman Wang back to his son's house.

The priest said that Jen had been "out looking" for woman Wang; but however strong Jen's desire might have been to have his wife back—whether because he missed her or because he was planning vengeance against her—he was not in fact entitled to keep her, because of the crime of flight and adultery she had committed. The law was complicated on this point. It did state clearly that a husband could divorce a wife on one of seven grounds: inability to bear sons, lascivious behavior, failure to serve her in-laws properly, talking too much, having a thievish nature, being overjealous, and suffering from serious illness. (Divorce by mutual consent was also permitted under the law.) If the wife did not want the divorce, the husband was not allowed to divorce her if one of these three factors applied: the wife had mourned her husband's parents for three years; the husband had risen from poverty to riches during the time of his marriage; the wife had no family of her own to go to. Since woman Wang did not have a family living that she could return to, the law seemed at first glance to show that she should stay with Jen despite her infidelity; but a substatute added in the Ming stated specifically that the three exemptions from divorce did not apply if the woman had been adulterous. Since another clause of the *Legal Code* also stipulated that a husband would be beaten with eighty blows if he refused to send away his wife after she had committed an act for which she should have been divorced, it appears that technically Jen could have been punished for taking her back. But in fact nobody in the county administration took any action, nor did Jen follow any of the legal channels open to him. He did not start divorce proceedings. He did not arrange to sell woman Wang. He did not report her bad conduct to the local headman, so that her shame would be aired publicly, as he was entitled to do. Instead, he bought a new woven sleeping mat to lay upon the straw that served as their bed.

The two of them lived together again, in their house outside Kuei-ch'ang market, through the last months of 1671 and into January 1672. They would have been cold, for the mean temperature in Shantung during January was in the twenties, and the houses of the poor were frail: the walls were of beaten earth, mud bricks, or kaoliang stalks; the few wooden supports were unshaped branches, often thin and crooked; roofs were thatched thinly with straw and reeds and were not true proof against either wind or rain. If there was fuel available, it was used primarily for cooking, and the warmth from the cooking fire was fed under the raised brick sleeping platform through a system of flues; this sleeping platform was covered with a layer of straw. In Jen's house it was here that he placed the new mat he bought for woman Wang's return.

On an evening toward the end of January 1672, the two of them sat at home. Jen had told woman Wang to mend his jacket, and she was darning it by the light of a lamp. Outside it was snowing. The neighbors could see the light of the lamp shining from their house, and later they heard the two of them quarreling. The neighbors could hear the anger in the voices, though they could not make out the words. They were still listening when the lamp went out.

Woman Wang took off her outer jacket and trousers and her heavy shoes. She drew, over her bound feet, a pair of worn bed shoes, with soft soles of red cotton. Her jacket was blue, her thinner under-trousers were white. She lay in these clothes on the mat in the straw, and Jen waited while she fell asleep.

I*n the world it is winter, but it is warm here. There are lotuses in bloom on the green waters of the winter lake, their scent reaches her on the wind, there are people trying to pick them, but the plants drift away as the boats approach. She sees the winter mountains covered in flowers. The room is dazzlingly bright, a path of white stones leads to the door, red petals are scattered over the white stones, a single branch of blossom pokes through the window.*

The branch stretches out over the table, the leaves are far apart, but the blossoms are pressed thickly together, they are not yet opened, they are like the wings of a butterfly, like the wings of a damp butterfly, moistened and hanging down; the stems that hold them to the branch are fine as hairs.

She can see how beautiful she is, the lines are gone from her face, her hands are smooth as a girl's, not rough from work. Her brows are dark and perfectly arched, her teeth are white and perfectly spaced, she practices her smile and the teeth just appear, she checks the corners of the lips and the corners of the eyes.

The sleeping place is covered with furs thick as palm fronds, they are deep and soft, the coverlet is filled with shreds of cotton and powdered incense, the chamber is filled with its fragrance. The man is handsome but he looks ill, his face is bathed with tears. She rubs his temples, she brushes the dust from his clothes, she wipes the tears from his eyes; she can feel on his body the

weals from his beatings and she rubs them gently with her fingers.
She unfastens the belt of his robe and slips her hand inside,
she massages him lightly with her fists, but he cannot move from
pain, there is a tumor growing out of his chest, it is as big as a
bowl and gnarled like the growth at the foot of a tree. She slips
a golden bracelet off her wrist and presses it down upon the
tumor, the flesh rises around the outside of the bracelet, but the
center of the tumor rises up through the metal, she draws a knife
with a fine blade from her robe and slices it gently around the
bracelet's edge. The dark blood gushes out onto the bed and
matting, she takes a red pill from her mouth and presses it into
the wound, as she presses into the wound it slowly closes.

She is tired. Her limbs feel delicate and heavy, her legs
straighten and bend as if she has no force, but the beautiful
women admire her, they cluster around her, their foreheads
bound in red silk bands, their robes violet with sashes of green.
They carry bows and quivers on their backs, they have been out
hunting.

She passes through door after door until they reach the court-
yard. The trees are tall enough to reach the red eaves of the build-
ings, the court is full of flowers, and the seed pods are drifting
down off the trees in the light breeze, a swing is hanging down
on slack cords. They are helping her up into the swing, she stands
erect on the swing and reaches up her arms to hold the ropes,
she is wearing a short-sleeved dress and her arms are shining, the
ropes of the swing are hanging from the clouds, her dark hair
swirls around her neck, she stretches up with her bright arms and
light as a swallow swings up into the clouds.

There is a boat of many colors drifting toward her in the sky,
it is draped with fine clouds. People are climbing aboard. There
is only one oarsman, he holds a short wooden oar. The oar has no
blade at the end, the end is thickly clustered with feathers like a
giant fan; as the oarsman waves the feathers a light wind blows
and they move ever faster through the clouds. There is no sound

but the throbbing of the light wind. The clouds are all around, they press in on her like cotton wool, they are soft under her feet, and she is slightly dizzy as though still traveling on the boat. She looks up and sees the stars close to her eyes, they range in size from great jars down to tiny cups, they are neatly arranged like the seeds within a lotus flower; below is an infinite silver sea, through gaps in the clouds she sees whole cities big as beans.

In front of her is a flight of steps, the steps are shining like rock crystal, she is reflected in each step as in a mirror. Clear water is running over white sand. There are little pavilions with red windows, there are beautiful women moving in the pavilions, and young men in embroidered coats and red shoes. People are eating fruit from jade bowls, they are drinking wine from goblets a foot around the rim. The peonies are ten feet high, the camellias twice as high again. A girl with white fingers plays an instrument she has never seen before, another plucks a lute with an ivory plectrum and sings of women who weep. As the music sounds a light breeze blows, birds crowd into the courtyard and settle quietly in the trees.

She sits down at the foot of a high tree. The trunk of the tree is wide and smooth, a single thread of yellow sap courses through its center, the leaves grow thickly on its delicate branches. It casts a deep shade. Red blossoms shimmer among the leaves and tinkle like precious stones as they fall. A bird is singing in the tree. Its feathers are gold and green. It is a strange bird, its tail is as long as its body, and the song it sings is a sad song that makes her think of home.

She moves away on high, scented shoes with hurried steps through the morning dew, the dew makes her shoes and stockings glossy with moisture. The trees are growing thickly, but through the trees she can see the tower, the walls are of copper, there are tall pillars of iron supporting a shimmering roof. There are no doors or windows in the walls but there are deep indentations, placed close together, and she climbs up by placing her feet in these. Inside she is quiet, she is safe.

He kneels beside her. He is trembling and hugs his own body with his arms. "Eat this," she says, and with her bare feet she treads the delicacies into the ground. "Over here," she says, and he offers her the night-soil bucket, holding it out for her in his hands. "Clean these," she says, and gives him her tiny embroidered shoes, caked with mud.

She places a woman's cap on his head, with her make-up she paints his face, she paints his face like a warrior's. There is a light cotton football, she kicks it into the air and he scampers after it, the sweat is pouring off him. The ball is transparent and filled with a glittering substance, he kicks it up in a shining arc through the air, it whistles through the air like a comet, it falls into the water, its light goes out in the water with a gurgle. And she sees that there is no tower, there are no round walls supporting a shimmering roof, there is no forest; there is only a cheap ring lying on the ground, needles thrust through it on which the lid of a make-up box is resting, all lying abandoned among the briers.

He stands before her in his ragged clothes, the snot is dribbling down his face, he smiles at her. "Does the pretty lady love me?" he asks. He hits her. The crowd presses closer to watch. He rolls a ball from his snot and gives it to her. "Eat it," he says. She puts it in her mouth and tries to swallow, he laughs aloud, "The pretty lady loves me," he cries. She wants to answer but her mouth is full of earth, she is pinned, she is pinned by the snake's coils that enfold her, she struggles harder, her body is thrashing in the water, she can smell the filth in the water, the people are crowded along the river bank, they are watching and laughing, they must help her, she must cry out, they will not help her

As Jen's hands drove deeply into her neck, woman Wang reared her body up from the bed, but she could not break free. His hands stayed tight around her throat and he forced his knee down onto her belly to hold her still. Her legs thrashed with such force that she shredded the sleeping mat, her bowels opened, her feet tore through the mat to the straw beneath, but his grip never slackened and none of the neighbors heard a sound as woman Wang died.

It was still snowing in T'an-ch'eng. Jen picked up his wife's body and drew her blue outer jacket around her shoulders. He opened the door and began to carry her through the woods, toward the house of his neighbor Kao. This was how he had planned it: when she was dead he would take her body to Kao's house and leave it in the gateway; he would say she had been having an adulterous affair with Kao and that Kao had killed her. The story would be plausible: she had already run away once, and Kao was a violent and quick-tempered man. The two of them could have been carrying on every day while Jen was away at work.

But Jen never reached Kao's house with woman Wang. As he walked through the dark wood a dog barked. Watchmen, sheltering in the porch, banged a warning gong. A light shone. Jen dropped the body in the snow and waited. No one came to investigate. The light went out and there was silence again. He left woman Wang lying where she was and returned to his empty house, locked the door, and went to sleep.

The body of woman Wang lay out in the snow all night. When she was found she looked almost alive: for the intense cold had preserved, in her dead cheeks, a living hue.

Epilogue: The Trial

THE TRIAL took four days.

On the first day, early in the morning, Jen and his father made their way on foot to the magistrate's yamen in T'an-ch'eng city and filed a formal complaint against their neighbor Kao for having had an adulterous relationship with woman Wang and subsequently murdering her. Such charges had to be properly written out, and certified scribes were available to help the illiterate, for a fee. In an attempt to prevent corruption or distortion at this the earliest stage of any trial, the scribes were licensed and expected to provide their own guarantors. Jen's formal statement ran: "Late last night I told my wife woman Wang to darn my inner jacket; I blew out the lamp and went to sleep. Later I heard the sound of the door closing and got up to take a look, but all I could see was my wife walking away, with Kao holding a knife and following behind her. Kao's wife, woman Ts'ao, was standing by the gate of their house, holding a lamp and waiting for them. I was afraid he'd kill me, so I didn't dare go after them; I came home, closed the door, and went to bed."

The deposition was checked for errors by the clerks in the yamen, and the same clerks checked that Jen was there in person and had not sent a substitute; then the deposition was registered, sealed, and sent in to the magistrate's inner yamen to be read by the magistrate in person. Huang Liu-hung read the charge, and sent out police runners to arrest Kao and his wife. (If the charge had been less serious, he would have issued a temporary warrant and sent Jen off with it to make his own arrest of Kao, and order him to appear in court.) Kao and his wife were brought back under escort to T'an-ch'eng and placed in the city prison, a small group of buildings in the southeast corner of the magistrate's compound.

Had the Kaos been left for any protracted time in prison, Jen would have considered it adequate recompense for the insult he had received in the temple when Kao had struck him two months before, without any need to have them tried and punished. The prison world was a grim one, often fatal for the poor, who could not afford to pay off the jailers, and extremely costly for the wealthy. Huang Liu-hung wrote with regret of the practices he knew went on: jailers torturing prisoners by beating them, chaining them too tightly, forcing them to stand all night, even soaking their bedding or flooding their cells with water, all in the aim of forcing them to pay protection; prisoners beating up their fellows in reprisal, or stealing their food, or forcing wealthier prisoners to have food sent in for all; officials killing prisoners so they could keep the objects they had stolen, or killing a major criminal out of fear that he might escape. Huang could offer only advice on watchfulness and fairness, regular health inspections and exercise, careful separation of women prisoners from the men, and the development of a mutual security system, modeled after the *pao-chia* system of registration in the outer world, in which prisoners were divided into groups of five, with each being made responsible for the other four in alternating five-day cycles. But on the night after the Kaos were arrested, Huang Liu-hung happened to have dinner with an acquaintance of his named Hsieh, who was leaving to take up a junior post elsewhere. In casual conversation Hsieh mentioned that the people in Kuei-ch'ang were talking about the case with some excitement, and were angry and puzzled that Kao should have killed woman Wang after having had an affair with her. After hearing Hsieh's comments, Huang felt it would be wise to look carefully into the case right away.

On the second day, at noon, the trial began. The Jens, as the plaintiffs, knelt on the east side of the hall, the Kaos on the west side, for the accused. The gates were locked; one clerk was ready to take transcriptions of the testimony. Jen repeated his story—that he had been asleep when he heard a sound at the door, and saw woman Wang leaving the house with Kao just behind her, holding a knife. Through the trees he could see Kao's wife, woman Ts'ao, waiting for the couple; she was leaning against the doorway, holding a lantern. Jen, afraid that he would be killed if he went after them, returned to bed. Rising at dawn, he found his wife lying dead in the woods. He immediately ran to alert his father, told him what he had seen, and came with him to prefer the formal charges.

Had the woman been beaten to death or stabbed, asked the magistrate?

"It was still too dark to see clearly," answered Jen.

Other villagers, questioned about the killing, pleaded ignorance.

Kao was questioned about his role in the case. Though the magistrate deliberately shouted at him in feigned anger, and had Kao surrounded by yamen runners holding the heavy boards that were often used to squeeze a prisoner's ankles in order to extort confessions, Kao stuck to his story. He admitted having seen woman Wang in the temple two months before and having struck Jen in the face after their argument, but he denied any adultery with woman Wang and denied that he had killed her. Indeed, he said that though he did live near the Jens, they had never had social relations.

Kao's wife, woman Ts'ao, corroborated her husband's story and added further details that provided a convincing alibi for him: late that night she had been steaming the dumplings for the new year's festival in her kitchen area when she heard a gong beating just outside her door. Going out to see what was happening, she found the village night watchmen sheltering from the cold inside her covered gateway; they had lit a fire and were smoking tobacco. She returned inside and bolted the door. Her husband, all this time, was peacefully sleeping.

Huang Liu-hung was impressed by the sincerity of their testimony and found Jen's story increasingly odd. He ordered both Jen and his father put in prison for the night, released Kao and his wife on pledges of security (*ya-pao*); after court was dismissed, Huang sent off his runners with an urgent red warrant to find out which men had been on watch in woman Wang's village on the night in question and to order them to report the following morning for questioning.

On the third day Huang rode out with some attendants to the village near Kuei-ch'ang market and asked to be shown the Jens' house. He noted its extreme poverty, the few possessions, the rips in the almost new mat that lay on the straw bed, and a pile of dried excrement by the bed. In answer to his questions, his retainers said that the poor people in the area burned oxen and donkey dung for fuel; still puzzled, Huang ordered some water boiled, and the dung placed in a hole scooped in the earth floor. When the boiling water was poured on the dung the watchers could tell by the odor that the source was human, not animal. Huang also questioned woman Wang's neighbors, including a ten-year-old girl who had heard the Jens quarreling. None of them had any information to offer about the killing.

Woman Wang's body still lay in the wood, in the snow, though someone had thrown a little loose earth over her. Huang had the body lifted out; he noted the details of her clothes, and the faded red cotton bed shoes on her bound feet. Since it was improper for a man to touch her body, he ordered an old woman brought from the village to search woman Wang's body for wounds. After a brief examination she reported that there were none. Huang told her to look more carefully and overcome her distaste for stretching out the limbs, now frozen in place by the cold and rigor mortis; this second search revealed massive bruises on both sides of the neck and, when the old woman had stripped down the clothes, a massive bruise on the lower belly.

In the meantime the village watchmen had been assembled at Kao's house, and they admitted that because of the cold they had not been patrolling but had lit a fire and sheltered in the Kaos' outer doorway. About midnight they thought they had seen someone moving around in the wood and they heard a dog begin to bark; in case it might have been a robber, they beat their gong to scare him away. Kao's wife, hearing the noise, had come out to ask them what was going on; they explained, and she returned inside. They knew nothing about woman Wang's death and had seen no one else. They scattered to their homes at dawn, in the fifth watch—apparently none of them had noticed the body lying in the snow.

Returning to T'an-ch'eng city, Huang decided to use a technique that he had found successful before, using fear of the City God to compel the telling of the truth by frightened witnesses. He told one of the youngsters on his household staff to hide in the small room at the back of the City God's temple and to take note of anything that either Jen or his father might say during the night. When the boy was concealed, Jen and his father were brought by the police runners from the prison to the main hall of the City God's temple, where they were chained, some distance apart, to two pillars. While the two men looked on, Huang burned incense before the god and prayed: "Last night the City God told me the reasons for the death of Jen's wife, and now I understand; but there are still some aspects of the circumstances of her death that I do not understand exactly, and I beg the God to enlighten me." The prayer ended, Huang urged the two Jens to repent and criticize themselves before the god, and left them there alone for the night.

The fourth day Huang had the Jens returned to prison and

questioned the youngster about their conversation. Though the father had repeatedly asked his son how woman Wang had died, said the boy, Jen had never given a clear answer, nor had he made any more remarks about Kao. He had merely said, over and over again, that it was he, Jen, who deserved to die.

Convinced now that Kao, woman Ts'ao, and the father Jen were all innocent, Huang summoned Jen to court. Since Jen would still not confess, Huang offered him his reconstruction of the crime: the quarrel, the strangling, the knee in the stomach, the body carried out into the snow, the sudden glimpse of woman Ts'ao in the light of the watchmen's fire that gave Jen the idea of implicating her, too. Jen kowtowed, and gave his confession, which was recorded by the clerks; in the confession he admitted that Huang's reconstruction was correct.

By Ch'ing law, both Jen and his father should have received the death penalty for falsely accusing an innocent person of a capital crime. But Huang found massive mitigating circumstances. In the first place, the father had known nothing about the crime; second, he was over seventy and Jen was his only son; third, Jen himself had no children, so the family line would certainly die out if he was executed; fourth, woman Wang had not followed the *tao* of a wife—she had betrayed her husband and had deserved to die; fifth, Jen had indeed been provoked in the temple by Kao, who should never have hit him.

Accordingly, Jen's father was exonerated, and Jen was sentenced to be beaten with the heavy bamboo and to wear the cangue around his neck for a lengthy period of time. Such beatings could lead to death, as Huang well knew, since on at least two occasions he had had prisoners beaten in his yamen: one had died a month after receiving thirty blows, another after ten days. Wearing the cangue, moreover, was a major humiliation that Huang reserved for those deserving public shame. But if Jen survived the beating and could live with the shame, he would be free to follow the dictates of filial piety and look after his aged father. A further presumption, in view of the talk about family lines not dying out and Jen's being the only child, seems to have been that Jen would marry again if he could find a bride.

Though she was dead, woman Wang still posed a problem, perhaps more of a problem than she had ever posed in her life. For in life she had not had the power to hurt anybody, except her father-in-law and husband by her language and conduct, and perhaps the man she ran away with. But dead and vengeful she was suffused with power and danger: as a hungry ghost she could roam the village for generations, impossible to placate, impossible to exorcise. That woman T'ien was still living shows how seriously such arguments were taken in T'an-ch'eng: thirty years before, as a young widow, she had threatened to kill herself and become a ghost haunting the Hsü home if she was not granted her wish to live out a single life, and she had got her way. Huang's decision was that woman Wang should be buried in a good coffin, in a plot of land near her home; if this was done, he felt, then "her lonely spirit would be pacified." For this purpose he allocated ten taels—a sizable sum, since on similar occasions Huang had granted no more than three taels to placate the dead. But Huang himself did not wish to put up the money; nor could the Jen family afford to bury woman Wang in such style even had they wanted to. Accordingly, he told the neighbor Kao to pay for the land and the funeral expenses: that would both take care of woman Wang and teach Kao not to hit people in the face when he lost his temper.

Notes

❋

FENG: *T'an-ch'eng hsien-chih* 郯城縣志 [Local History of T'an-ch'eng], chief editor and writer Feng K'o-ts'an 馮可參 , 10 chuan, editor's preface dated 1673. Later editions by different editors appeared in 1763 and 1810, and are cited accordingly as *T'an-ch'eng hsien-chih* (1763) and *T'an-ch'eng hsien-chih* (1810).

HUANG: *Fu-hui ch'üan-shu* 福專全書 [A Complete Book Concerning Happiness and Benevolence] by Huang Liu-hung 黃六鴻, author's preface 1694. Compiled in a new edition by Yamane Yukio 山根幸夫 (following edition by Obata Yukihiro 小畑行蘭). Kyoto, 1974.

P'U: *Liao-chai chih-i* 聊齋志異 [Strange Stories Written in the Liao Studio] by P'u Sung-ling 蒲松齡 , author's preface 1679. I use the complete edition, with commentaries, based on P'u's original manuscript, edited by Chang Yu-hao 張友鶴, and titled *Liao-chai chih-i, hui-chiao, hui-chu, hui-p'ing pen* . . . 會校會注會評本. 3 vols., Shanghai, 1962.

PREFACE

The broadest studies of pre-modern rural China (in English) are Hsiao Kung-chuan, *Rural China: Imperial Control in the Nineteenth Century,* and Ho Ping-ti, *Studies on the Population of China, 1368–1953.* A valuable study of the transitional period before the establishment of the People's Republic is Ramon Myers, *The Chinese Peasant Economy: Agricultural Development in Hopei and Shantung, 1890–1949* (Cambridge, Mass.: Harvard University Press, 1970).

Among excellent local studies are: Susan Naquin, *Millenarian Rebellion in China: The Eight Trigrams Uprising of 1813* (New Haven: Yale University Press, 1976); James Cole, "Shaohsing: Studies in Ch'ing Social History" (Ph.D. dissertation, Stanford University, 1975); the essays by Frederic Wakeman, Jerry Dennerline, and James Polachek in Frederic Wakeman and Carolyn Grant, eds., *Conflict and Control in Late Imperial China* (Berkeley: University of California Press, 1975); Jonathan Ocko, "Ting Jih-ch'ang and Restoration Kiangsu, 1864–1870: Rhetoric and Reality" (Ph.D. dissertation, Yale University, 1975); and Hilary Beattie, "Land and Lineage in China: A Study of T'ung-ch'eng County, Anhwei, in the Ming and Ch'ing Dynasties" (Ph.D. dissertation, Cambridge University, 1973).

Though it would be pointless here to assemble a bibliography of medieval Western local studies, I am thinking of such works (parallel in topical range to my own, but immensely more detailed) as Barbara Hanawalt, "Violent Death in Fourteenth- and Early Fifteenth-Century England," *Comparative Studies in Society and History* 18:3 (1976), 297–320, or the prospectus by Pierre Chaunu, "Mourir à Paris, XVIe, XVIIe, XVIIIe siècles," *Annales* 31:1 (1976), 29–31.

Huang Liu-hung's memoir and handbook, entitled the *Fu-hui ch'üan-shu,* which means literally "A Complete Book Concerning Happiness and Benevolence," has an author's preface dated 1694. Huang Liu-hung referred to one other local handbook as having been particularly useful to him as a model; that was the *Wei-hsin pien* by P'an Shao-ts'an, written during the mid-1670s and published in 1684. (See Huang's own "Fan-li," p. 5, and the third page of Yamane Yukio's introduction to Huang's *Fu-hui ch'üan-shu.*) Huang also admired Li Yü's anthology of administrative studies, the *Tzu-chih hsin-shu* (first printed in 1663, expanded edition 1667), as he tells us in HUANG 229d. For a list of the major magistrates' handbooks, see John Watt, *The District Magistrate in Late Imperial China* (New York: Columbia University Press, 1972), pp. 267–68, note 56.

Fuller references to the works of P'u Sung-ling are given in the notes to Chapter I, "The Observers," below.

Apart from some brief pieces in the various Local Histories the only reference I have come across that specifically praises T'an-ch'eng is in an essay by Chao Meng-an, "T'an-ch'eng I-nan shih-she," published in early 1977; here Chao recalls the famous poetry groups of Ma-t'ou market in the late Ch'ing, and reflects favorably on the scenery along the I river near T'an-ch'eng. The essay is tinged by the nostalgia of a writer, now living in Taiwan, for his Chinese home county.

ONE: THE OBSERVERS

1. Earthquake: FENG 9/12–13.

2. "Throwing rocks": FENG 3/7.

2. Natural cycles: FENG preface, and *lun* to 1585 edition cited 5/12b–13, 9/15.

2–3. Feng biography: *Shao-wu fu-chih* 20/22. His degrees are listed in ibid. 7/2–3, and the preface shows he had been on the compiler's staff of the Shao-wu gazetteer while he was magistrate in T'an. For his invitation to compile the T'an-ch'eng history, see his own introduction. The Tu and Hsü, mentioned below as having passed the *chü-jen* degree, were both dead by the time Feng took up office in T'an-ch'eng.

3. T'an-ch'eng statistics: FENG 3/6b on details; 3/34 for *ting*, using a 1:6 ratio as on 9/12b; 3/7b–8b on land (*Ch'ing* divided by 100, times 6); 9/17 on townships (i.e., 32 and 13 *li*, totaling 45). Comparable figures for other areas of Shantung are given by Fujita Keiichi, "Shinshō Santō," pp. 128–31.

4. White Lotus: FENG 9/8 has immediate local effects. Details on leaders and their promises are in *Tsou-hsien-chih* 3/81–83, which also gives local leaders' places of origin. There are also extensive commentaries in P'U 34, and sources on the White Lotus are well marshaled in Chan, "The White Lotus," p. 226, n. 1. A more detailed account of the Shantung rising is in Richard Chu, "The White Lotus Sect," pp. 115–23.

4. Locusts: FENG 9/9.

5. 1641 raids: Led by Shih Erh and Yao San from northwest Shantung, FENG 9/9b–10. More detail on these two leaders is in *Pi-hsien-chih* 5/7b and *Tsou-hsien-chih* 3/84b.

5. Wang Ying: *T'an-ch'eng hsien-chih* (1763) 8/18b and 9/9b.

5–6. Defense of T'an-ch'eng: List of 292 men, *T'an-ch'eng hsien-chih* (1810) 127–29; collated with degree purchasers, FENG 8/10–11; total list, *T'an-ch'eng hsien-chih* (1810) 127–56, nineteen names indecipherable; discovery of tablet discussed, ibid. 369–70.

6. April attack: *T'an-ch'eng hsien-chih* (1810) 349; FENG 9/9b–10. The brothels of Hung-hua are mentioned in P'U 220.

6–7. 1643 attack: FENG 9/10—the jen-wu year is mainly in 1642, but the twelfth month corresponds to January 1643. One can assess 1641 survivors killed in 1643 by collating the list of defenders in *T'an-ch'eng hsien-chih* (1810) with the dead men listed in lieh-nü chuan, FENG, chuan 7.

6–7. Abatai's raid: *Shih-lu* (T'ai-tsung) pp. 1046–47, 1072, 1075–76. (Among the officers was Oboi, future regent of China.) Abatai's route in Shantung can be traced in T'an Ch'ien's *Kuo-chüeh*, pp. 5948, 5954, 5955, 5956 (where he gives February 18, 1643, as the date of the sack of T'an-ch'eng), and 5971. Effects of the raid were felt as far east as Hai-chou, as can be seen from the chronology and biographies in *Hai-chou chih-li-chou chih*, pp. 68–69, 428–29. A brief biography of Abatai is in Arthur Hummel, ed., *Eminent Chinese of the Ch'ing Period*, pp. 3–4. He was the seventh son of Nurhaci. A detailed biography with descriptions of this and the other great raids Abatai led is in *Pa-ch'i t'ung-chih*, chuan 132, pp. 1–16. Only a year after the great Manchu raid, advance parties of Li Tzu-ch'eng's armies extracted half a million taels easily enough from the Shantung populace and were moving to a graded levy (from 100,000 for board presidents, 10,000 for lesser officials, and 100 for lower degree holders) before they were routed by the main Manchu armies; obviously the Manchus had merely tapped the immense source of private wealth that was generally kept concealed. See Li Wen-chih, *Wan-Ming min-pien*, p. 143.

7–8. Year 1644: *T'an-ch'eng hsien-chih* (1810) 156; FENG 9/10b.

8. Floods: FENG 9/11.

9. Bandit victims: Woman Yao, FENG 7/27b; woman Sun, 7/25b–26; Tu Chih-tung, 9/11 and 7/6b (*chü-jen* lists 8/4b–5). For problems in identifying the dead, see *T'an-ch'eng hsien-chih* (1810) 157–58. The bandit groups can be tracked through *Ko-tse-hsien hsiang-t'u-chih* 28–29; *I hsien-chih* 1/27; *Tsou hsien-chih* 3/86.

9–12.   Locals reply to Huang: HUANG 63c.

12.   T'an-ch'eng worse off: HUANG 74c.

12.   Granaries: "I-ts'ang," FENG 5/12; refusal to loan grain, ibid. 5/15.

12.   Schools: "She-hsüeh" and "I-hsüeh," FENG 5/7. Refusal to rebuild schools, HUANG 295b. A description of the ideal school system, class procedures, and support systems is in ibid. 296a and b. The Shantung school-land system during the Ch'ing dynasty is studied in detail in Nakamura Jihei's two articles in *Shien* (February 1955 and December 1956).

12–13.   Ruins: Walls, FENG 2/1b–2; physician, 2/3; bridge, 2/8; temples, 4/6b.

13.   Huang biography: *T'an-ch'eng hsien-chih* (1763) 7/26–27; Wang Chih, "T'an-ch'eng Yin Huang Ssu-hu chuan" (Wang Chih was magistrate of T'an-ch'eng from 1747 to 1749); Ch'en Wan-nai, *Hung Sheng yen-chiu*, pp. 125–127 (where Ch'en argues that as censor Huang was responsible for reporting Hung Sheng to the authorities in 1689); *Tung-kuang hsien-chih* 5/9. Huang's final rank was *Chi-shih-chung;* Brunnert and Hagelstrom number 210B.

13.   Government response: *Shih-lu*, K'ang-hsi reign, p. 385, report on earthquake ordered; p. 401, first earthquake rebates granted; p. 459, final 227,000-tael rebate for I-chou earthquake area. Lowered quotas: FENG 3/1b, 3/7b–8 and *T'an-ch'eng hsien chih* (1763) 5/18b.

14.   On T'an-ch'eng: HUANG 172c.

14–15.   Proclamation: HUANG 172d. He uses *kalpa*, which I translate as "cosmic cycle."

15–16.   Superstitions: FENG 3/36b, and his biography in *Shao-wu fu-chih* 20/22.

15–16.   Yü: FENG 1/12 and 4/8. Tseng: ibid. 1/8 and 1/12b–13.

16.   Examination questions: Fa-shih-shan, *Ch'ing-pi shu-wen,* p. 61, for the Shantung exam questions in 1669. The full context of each test phrase can be found in Legge, *The Chinese Classics,* as follows: question one, I, *Analects,* VI, chap. 17 and 18, 190–91; question two, I, *Doctrine of the Mean,* XXXII, chap. 1 and 2, 430; question three, II, *Mencius,* II, 1/2/27, p. 195.

17. *Chü-jen* failures: *T'an-ch'eng hsien-chih* (1763) 8/5.

17. Moral Maxims: *Shih-lu*, K'ang-hsi reign, pp. 485–86 for text, and on propagation, p. 491.

17. T'an Confucianism: Legge, *The Chinese Classics*, V, *Ch'un Ts'ew*, 665–68. Essays discuss the incident in FENG 10/15 and 10/16, and in *T'an-ch'eng hsien-chih* (1763) 11/1. Skepticism is expressed in *T'an-ch'eng hsien-chih* (1810) 358–59 by an interlocutor who quite logically points out that Confucius could have talked with T'an-tzu in Lu, though the essay's author marshals counterarguments. Popular illustrations of the scenes are in Doré, *Recherches*, XIII, 18–19.

18. Confucian shrines: FENG 1/7, 2/7, 4/6.

18. Abandoned temples: HUANG 247d.

18–19. Moral collapse: HUANG 360c and d.

19. Earthquake: P'U 170–71; also Giles, *Strange Stories*, p. 416. The earthquake was much lighter in Tzu-ch'uan, where it wrecked 557 buildings and killed 4 people: *Tzu-ch'uan hsien-chih* 3/56.

20. P'u's themes: See P'U 1622 for I-chou; "Ta-niang," P'U 1391–97 has considerable detail on men captured by Manchus, and the women's attempts to hold onto their land. Other widows' travails are described in P'U 191, 324, 661, 699, 927, 1019, 1210, 1284. These can be compared with *Tzu-ch'uan hisien-chih* 3/55 for famines and 3/60 for the Manchus.

20–21. Story of Liu: P'U 881, "Liu Hsing"; di Giura 1601–02.

21. Tzu-ch'uan siege: *Tzu-ch'uan hsien-chih* 3/60b–61, and numerous biographies in ibid 6(hsia)/22b–32, under the "ting-hai" year. See also *Po-shan hsien-chih*, p. 125; Chang Chun-shu and Chang Hsüeh-lun, "The World of P'u Sung-ling's *Liao-chai chih-i*," p. 416, n. 66.

21–22. Troops and bandits: P'U 1527, beginning of story "Chang Shih-fu."

22. P'u and rebellions: Details on Yü Ch'i's rising are in *Lai-yang hsien-chih* 34/5b–6, and Hsieh Kuo-chen, *Ch'ing-ch'u nung-min*, pp. 113–16. On the executions and Chi-nan coffins, see P'U 477 and 482; piles of corpses, 70; flight to caves, 921; mixed classes, 920 and 991; gentry

bandits, 240; literatus and bandit's daughter, 971; "un-righteous men," 1267; bandit or prostitute, 1426; Shan-tung gang, 902–04.

22. T'eng and I bases: *Pi hsien-chih* 5/7b; *Tsou hsien-chih* 3/86. The general topography of this part of Shantung and the major nineteenth-century risings that occurred there are documented in Chang Yao, *Shantung chün-hsing chi-lüeh*, chuan 19 (for Tsou-hsien) and chuan 20 (for P'u's home area of Tzu-ch'uan). This work is a major source for Yokoyama Suguru's "Kampōki Santō no kōryō."

23. Fox rebel: P'u 1086, "Tou-hu"; Giles, *Strange Stories*, p. 373; di Giura 1386.

23–24. Medical medium: P'u 267–68, "K'ou-ch'i"; di Giura 1391–93. The sounds are an untranslatable study in onomatopoeia.

24–25. Medium Liang: P'u 691–92, "Shang-hsien"; di Giura 1681–83. For current shamanistic practices, see Jack M. Potter, "Cantonese Shamanism" in Wolf, ed., *Religion and Ritual*, pp. 207–31, especially pp. 215–17 on the "shrine where spirits reside."

25. P'u's life: Basic data are in Arthur Hummel, ed., *Eminent Chinese*, pp. 628–30, and Průšek, *Chinese History and Literature*. The most thorough chronological biography is by Lu Ta-huan, "P'u Liu-yüan hsien-sheng nien-p'u." A carefully annotated biography reconstructed from P'u's poems is Liu Chieh-p'ing's *Liao-chai pien-nien shih-chi hsüan-chu*. Recent photographs of P'u's original home, garden, and tomb are printed at the beginning of *P'u Sung-ling chi*.

There is a large body of Chinese literature on P'u Sung-ling's art and his political stance, much of which is use-fully summarized by Chang Chun-shu and Chang Hsüeh-lun in "The World of P'u Sung-ling's *Liao-chai chih-i*." Other valuable studies are Ho Man-tzu's *P'u Sung-ling yü "Liao-chai chih-i*," which discusses P'u's class stance and collates the stories with seven of P'u's later dramas; also Chang P'ei's essay on anti-Manchu elements in P'u in "*Liao-chai chih-i . . . min-tsu ssu-hsiang*" (which is a partial rejoinder to Ho Man-tzu); Chang Yu-hung's discussion in P'u 1727–28 of variants between the original manuscript and the Ch'ien-lung printed version; and Yang Liu's study of sources for different stories in his *"Liao-chai chih-i" yen-chiu.* The recently discovered draft manuscripts of P'u's *Liao-chai chih-i* are analyzed by Yang Jen-k'ai and by Chang Ching-ch'iao. Otto Ladstätter, "P'u Sung-ling," also has useful discussions on P'u's attitudes and language. Nineteen recent essays on P'u have been collected in *P'u Sung-ling yen-chiu tzu-liao.*

25–26.   P'u's wife: Adapted from the translation by Jaroslav Prušek, "Two Documents Relating to the Life of P'u Sung-ling," in Prušek, *Chinese History and Literature,* pp. 84–91, this section being from pp. 85–88. The original essay is in *P'u Sung-ling chi* 252–53.

27.   P'u alone at night: P'u, prefaces, p. 3, which gives extensive commentary on this dense and difficult passage. There is a partial translation by Hervouet, *Contes,* pp. 10–11, a thoroughly annotated one in Giles, *Strange Stories,* p. xv, and a recent complete translation in Chang and Chang, "The World of P'u Sung-ling's *Liao-chai chih-i,*" p. 418. "Tales of the Underworld" refers to the Sung work by Liu I-ch'ing, *Yu-ming lu.* P'u added a few more stories over the following years, but the collection was basically complete by 1679. On P'u's hardship in these years, see Jaroslav Prušek, "*Liao-chai chi-i* by P'u Sung-ling," in Prušek, *Chinese History and Literature,* pp. 92–108.

27–30.   Boyhood magic: P'u 32, di Giura 1387. Some texts insert the character "*shih,*" to "take an exam," at the beginning of the story. But the prefectural exams were not usually held in the spring, and P'u seems to have been younger than exam-taking age in this story. "Celebrating the spring" is "*yen-ch'un.*"

30–32.   The dream: P'u 739, di Giura 1878. This is one of P'u's later additions to his collection, dated 1683. I cease the translation at the point where P'u reconstructs, in highly elegant and allusive language, the draft he wrote for the Fairy.

32.   The man and two ladies: P'u 220–31. The location comes on 220, the circumstances of transmittal on 231.

TWO: THE LAND

33. Snow: FENG 9/15. Huang's horse: HUANG 68a, which describes conditions in K'ang-hsi's ninth year, twelfth month, twenty-fifth day. Snow welcomed: Yang, *Chinese Village*, pp. 17–18. I-chou precipitation levels are in Buck, *Statistics*, p. 1, table 3; temperatures, p. 7, table 5.

34. T'an-ch'eng county: FENG, chuans 1 and 2; the 1673 maps are poorly printed and list few places; no maps are given in later T'an-ch'eng gazetteers. One can work out locations, however, from the coordinates given in FENG 3/1–2b. In 1724 T'an-ch'eng was transferred from Yen-chou fu to I-chou: *Hui-tien shih-li* 5443.

34–35. Crops: The basic crops growing in T'an-ch'eng in 1673 are listed in FENG 3/33–34. These data can be collated with Buck, *Statistics*, passim, for the winter wheat/kaoliang areas; p. 261 shows main crop cycles. Buck, *Atlas*, pp. 3–7, shows T'an-ch'eng (no. 112) included under the neighboring county of Yi (no. 118).

35–36. Work cycle: Yang, *Chinese Village*, pp. 16–23, excluding the later Western imported crops peanuts and sweet potatoes. Buck, *Statistics*, passim, on Shantung winter-wheat villages; other Shantung precipitation and temperature figures are in both Mark Bell, *China*, pp. 45–47, and Buck, *Statistics*.

36. Tax table: HUANG 89c and d.

37. Subdivisions: FENG 3/2b gives a brief summary of the *li-chia* system. I translate *hsiang* as "districts," *li* and *she* as "townships." "Township head" is *she-ch'ang*. Each *hsiang* was headed by a *kung-cheng*. The *hu-t'ou* structure is elaborated in HUANG 84c and d. There are not enough data in FENG or HUANG to reconstruct all details of the local tax system, though there are rich data for other areas of Shantung in later periods. See particularly the materials assembled from documents and interviews by Ching Su and Lo Lun in their *Ch'ing-tai Shan-tung ching-ying ti-chu*, Ramon Myers, "Commercialization, Agricultural Development . . . in Shantung Province," and David Buck, "The Provincial Elite in Shantung during the Republican Period."

37–38. Tax gatherers: Ray Huang, *Taxation,* pp. 36–37, for Ming honorific examples. Yü Shun is listed, with others of the Yü surname, as a *she-ch'ang* in *T'an-ch'eng hsien-chih* (1810) 144, and his biography is in *T'an-ch'eng hsien-chih* (1763) 9/9b. HUANG 75d–76a suggests both Hus were *she-ch'ang* of Hsin-wang township, and the two-person system is also listed in *I-chou chih* 1/17. Flight from the office among *pao-chia* heads who faced similar problems is described in Hsiao, *Rural China,* pp. 80–81.

38. Population figures: *Ting* figures appear in FENG 3/2b and 3/7. There it is stated that of 8700 dead in the quake, 1552 were *ting;* following a similar ratio, the 9498 *ting* registered in 1670 should imply a total population of 55,000–65,000 when the exempted families are added in. The total population figures are approximations only; for problems in making such assessments, see Ho Ping-ti, *Population,* chap. 2; for parallel assessments in Shantung, see Fujita Keiichi, pp. 136–37.

38. Pao-chia: FENG 3/1–2; HUANG 244–45. Hsiao, *Rural China,* chap. 3. On pp. 265–66 Hsiao cites some of Huang's own views. The markets are in FENG 3/34b. The terminology used in HUANG shows that in the countryside of T'an-ch'eng a "household head" (*hu-ch'ang*) was responsible for his own lands and family, a *chia-ch'ang* for ten households, a *pao-cheng* for ten *chia-ch'ang* or one hundred households, and a *pao-ch'ang* for one of the four districts. I use "township" here for *li* and *she.*

38–39. Registration: HUANG 249, where *chü-jen* are not considered as *hsiang-shen.*

38–39. Militia: HUANG 250c, though his overall figures of 50 *hu* per *chuang* and 100 *chuang* per *hsiang* would apply only to counties larger than T'an-ch'eng.

39. Arrears: HUANG 89c.

39–40. Budget: Taxes, FENG 3/3b–11b; staff, 3/16–17b; military, 3/25; river works, 3/29. Rates are summarized in *T'an-ch'eng hsien-chih* (1763) 5/19–22. The proportions of service levies drawn from *ting* (56.6%) and from land (43.4%) for T'an-ch'eng in 1608 are given in Huang, *Taxation,* p. 130.

40. Roads: FENG 2/7–8.

40. Post stations: FENG 3/18–19 on costs, and discussion, 3/23–24. Huang Liu-hung got the system reformed in 1672: ibid. and reports in HUANG 71 and 72.
41. Corvée: HUANG 92c, and 354a for timber. Road distance to Peking, *T'an-ch'eng hsien-chih* (1763) 2/27b.
41. River corvée: Essay in FENG 3/29; also HUANG 74d–75a.
42. Lowered quotas: *T'an-ch'eng hsien-chih* (1763) 5/18b; FENG 3/1b, 3/7b–8b.
43. "Fiscal acres": See discussions in Huang, *Taxation,* pp. 40–42; in Ho Ping-ti, *Population,* pp. 102–23; and in Wang, *Land Taxation,* pp. 32–33. FENG 3/19 cites this view of the lowest rating from the Wan-li reign *Local History.*
43–44. "Sandy soil" cases: HUANG 68. Huang seems to be describing polder land, perhaps covered by extra alluvion.
44. Cheating: Assayers, HUANG 87b; grain taken, 99a; "city as hell," 83b.
44. Collection chests: HUANG 80a and 80c. In 81c, Huang suggests one box for each four *li.*
44–45. Other taxes: Objects to be furnished, FENG 3/20b and *T'an-ch'eng hsien fu-i ch'üan-shu.* Others are discussed in HUANG: peddlers, 102; brokers, 101b; pawnshops, 101a (these taxes were doubled in 1674 to pay for the San-fan war); tobacco and liquors, 101c; meltage fee, 87.
45–46. Fighting crickets: P'U 484; di Giura 689; Giles, *Strange Stories,* pp. 275–76.
46. Urban merchants: HUANG 73c and d for amounts collected, 74a and b on merchants, and note on Ma-t'ou, giving references to data on p. 119, below.
46. Market headmen: HUANG 74a and 70a.
47. Soldiers: HUANG 70a, 77b.
47. Contracts: HUANG 146d.
47–48. Landlord abuses: HUANG 106d–107b, FENG 3/15.
48. *Pao-lan* system: HUANG 107c–d, dividing gentry into *hsiang-shen* and *ch'ing-chin;* FENG 3/15b for Feng's list of abuses; Hsiao, *Rural China,* pp. 132–39. I take the translation "proxy remittance" (which seems the best of many variants) from an essay by Jerry Dennerline in Wakeman and Grant, *Conflict and Control.* The pattern

of early Ch'ing tax evasion by the gentry, and the problem of unregistered lands, are studied in detail by Nishimura Genshō in "Shinsho no tochi"; the violent protests that broke out in Shantung later in the Ch'ing have been analyzed by Yokoyama Suguru in "Kampōki Santō no kōryō."

49. City God: FENG 4/4. A general account of this god's activities and the honors paid to him is in Shryock, *Temples of Anking*, pp. 98–115; and discussion of his place in the local hierarchy in Arthur Wolf, "Gods, Ghosts, and Ancestors," in Wolf, *Religion and Ritual*, p. 139.

49–50. Locust prayer: HUANG 281a–c; dated at 1671 by evidence in following prayer. In P'U 491 P'u Sung-ling has a story of a successful appeal to the local god in the I-chou area.

50–56. "Hsiao-erh": P'U 378–82. This story can also be found in an excellent French translation in Hervouet, *Contes extraordinaires*, pp. 68–74; di Giura 590–96.

56. Glass factory: P'u Sung-ling probably got this idea from the glassworks (*Liu-li*) that was flourishing in the seventeenth century in the next-door county to Tzu-ch'uan, Po-shan. From his biographies we know P'u passed through Po-shan on his journeys. The manufactory is described in detail in *Po-shan hsien-chih* 572–76; the Gazetteer's source is Sung T'ing-ch'üan's work *Yen-shan tsa-chi*, first published in 1665. This and other seventeenth-century Shantung industries are discussed in *Shantung ti-fang-shih chiang-shou t'i-kang* 35–36, and in Ching Su and Lo Lun, *Ch'ing-tai shan-tung ching-ying* 24–29.

56. Gentry "face": HUANG 80b.

57. Hsin-wang: HUANG 75c, locations FENG 3/1–2.

57. Morale of taxpayers: HUANG 92c.

57. Two lineages: Based on ratios of purchased or advanced degrees by surname to township registration, as reconstructed from FENG 8/2 and 8/9b–12. From Kao-ts'e there were five Changs and four Lius.

57–58. Liu-Hus case: in HUANG 75d–76c, Huang prints two of the reports on this case that he sent up to the prefect.

THREE: THE WIDOW

59. Woman P'eng: The details of the case are contained in two reports submitted to his superiors by Huang Liu-hung in 1670, HUANG 143c–144c, and 144c–145c.

59–60. Model widows: P'eng, FENG 7/22; Li, 7/22b (her son was Tu Chih-tung, listed with other *chü-jen* in 8/4b–5; his biography is in 7/6); Tu, 7/24; Liu, 7/25; T'ien, 7/30; Fan, 7/29b–30.

60–61. Old widow story: P'u 1221, "Chi nü"; di Giura 1212–13.

61. P'u's mockery: As in the story about scholar Tsung, P'u 682, part of which is translated in chap. 5 below, pp. 104–105.

61. Historiography: Feng's preface in FENG 3b–4. The compilers Tu, Liang, Chang, and Hsu were related respectively to Ch'en Shih, FENG 7/22b; Liu Shih, 7/25; Yang Shih, 7/23b; T'ien Shih and Tu Shih, 7/24b.

62. Widow and lover: P'u 699–703, "Chin sheng ssu."

62. Widows' intelligence: The best example is in P'u 1391–1401, "Ch'iu ta-niang," where a young widow leaves her own son with her late husband's family and returns to her native place in order to help her widowed mother hold on to the family land and bring up her two sons.

62–70. "Hsi-liu": P'u 1019–25; di Giura 966–73.

70. Other stories in P'u: Neighbors take widow's possessions, 1210, 1284; lawsuits and coercion, 672, 878, 907, 975, 1391; sexual excesses, 308, 668, 757, 1417, 1428; gambling, 532, 1270, 1473, 1534.

70. Widow Wu: FENG 7/20b. On "I" adoption across blood lines, see Boulais, *Manuel*, pp. 186–87 (section 386).

70–71. Widow An: FENG 7/21.

71. Widow Kao: FENG 7/28b–29.

71–72. Inheritance laws: *Tu-li ts'un-i*, p. 247 (clause 078.02); Staunton, *Penal Code*, p. 526, appendix 12A. The *Code* states that childless widows inherited their share of the husband's property and forfeited that when they remarried; status of a widow with children remarrying would vary, depending on whether she took the children with her like woman Wu, above, or abandoned them to her husband's family. P'u Sung-ling has a fictional example of such

abandonment in P'u 927, "Niu Ch'eng-chang." For husbands' ambivalences about their wives' remarriages, see
ibid. 96 and 191; and fear that children will be mistreated
by stepparents after remarriage in 1024 and 1322.

72–75. Ch'ens' harassment: HUANG 145a. For stealing oxen as a
crime, see *Tu-li ts'un-i*, p. 677 (clause 270.06). On the ox
in Shantung farms, see Yang, *Chinese Village*, p. 48, and
pp. 144–45, for curriculum and conduct in a poor village
school.

73. Choosing an heir: *Tu-li ts'un-i*, p. 247 (clause 078.02);
Boulais, *Manuel*, p. 189 (section 398).

73. Lien's uncle: HUANG 145a–b; Boulais, *Manuel*, pp. 188
and 190 (sections 393 and 400).

74–75. Vengeance clause: *Tu-li ts'un-i*, p. 962 (clause 323.00);
Boulais, *Manuel*, pp. 624–25 (sections 1444–46; in section 1448 Boulais lists a later case in which a son avenged
his mother after a lapse of ten years); Staunton, *Penal
Code*, pp. 352–53 (section 323).

75. The killing of Lien: HUANG 145b–c.

76. Striking a relative: *Tu-li ts'un-i*, p. 930 (clause 317.00);
Boulais, *Manuel*, pp. 611–12 (section 1410); Staunton,
Penal Code, pp. 344–45 (section 317).

FOUR: THE FEUD

77–78. P'u's family: *P'u Sung-ling chi,* p. 252; translated by
Prušek, "Two Documents Relating to the Life of P'u
Sung-ling," in Prušek, *Chinese History and Literature*, p.
86. (I have used pronouns instead of P'u's third-person
formality and tried to clarify the passage.)

78. Family fights: P'u 1580–87 "Tseng Yu-yü"; Giles, *Strange
Stories*, pp. 193–201. P'u has a story hinging on these
same rumors of girls being taken to Shun-chih's court in
P'u 1292.

79–89. "Ts'ui Meng": P'u 1127–34; di Giura 1289–98. This
story has many echoes from heroic tales and episodes of
the *Shui-hu-chuan* (*Water Margin*) type, and is not particularly typical of P'u's narrative style. The influence of
Shui-hu-chuan on Shantung inhabitants in the late Ming
is discussed by Chu, "White Lotus," pp. 115–16.

89. Wang San: HUANG 197b for Wang's past life and various alternate names. Details of the Yü Ch'i rising are in *Lai-yang hsien-chih* (*chuan-mo, fu-chi* section), pp. 5b–6. P'u Sung-ling has the rising as a focus for various stories, i.e., "Yeh-kou," P'u 70, and "Kung-sun chiu-niang," 477.

90. Li Tung-chen: The case is detailed in two lengthy reports by Huang Liu-hung, in HUANG 140a–141d and 196d–200a.

90–91. The quarrel: HUANG 140b, 197c. Yang, *Chinese Village,* pp. 169–70, discusses the crucial importance of a public insult in a rural Shantung community if it led to "loss of face."

91. The killings: HUANG 140c–141a.

92. The complaint: For another robbery and killing out of vengeance, see FENG 7/25, where robbers "ch'ou-tsei" the licentiate husband of Sun Shih during their 1650 raid on Kuei-ch'ang. "Ch'ou-tsei" is not a separate category in the robbery-with-violence part of the *Ch'ing Code*; see *Tu-li ts'un-i,* pp. 589–622 (clause 266).

92. Wang guarantor: HUANG 197c.

92. Twenty-four ruffians: Described in HUANG 39c and d. There are further parallels here with the Shantung world of the novel *Shui-hu-chuan* (*Water Margin*): Sung Chiang was a yamen clerk when he heard of the magistrate's plan to arrest the rebels, and so was able to warn them; Li K'uei was a guard in the Chiang-chou jail. See Irwin, *Evolution of a Chinese Novel,* pp. 123 and 132.

92–93. Yü Piao: HUANG 197c and d.

93–94. Kuan Ming-yü: HUANG 197d–198a.

94–95. Magistrate's resources: troops, FENG 3/17b–25; staff and their wages, FENG 3/16b–17b; cavalry to infantry ratios are in *T'an-ch'eng hsien-chih* (1763) 4/16b–17. The abilities of Lieutenant Chu Ch'eng-ming are described by Huang in HUANG 70d. I assume this is the same man as the Chu "Chün" of this case. Grooms vs. soldiers is in HUANG 70c. Condition of the horses that summer, HUANG 40c.

95. Journey to Chung-fang: HUANG 198b. An astonishing example of Huang's precision can be seen in his remark that the sixth lunar month in this particular year had only

twenty-nine instead of thirty days, so that the first day of the seventh lunar month was the "next day" to the twenty-ninth; the lunar calendar glossaries show that this was indeed the case in K'ang-hsi's ninth year.

96–97. The battle: HUANG 198c–199b.

97. Arrest and panic: HUANG 199c–d.

98. Killing three in a family: *Tu-li ts'un-i*, p. 815 (clause 287); Staunton, *Penal Code*, p. 308 (section 287); Boulais, *Manuel*, p. 551 (section 1249).

98. Wang's base in P'ei: HUANG 199b.

FIVE: THE WOMAN WHO RAN AWAY

99–100 The women's biographies: Those for the Ming and early Ch'ing are printed in FENG 7/19–30b.

100. Woman Kao's example: FENG 7/19b–20. An extraordinary example of the use of the City God's temple for a ritual declaration and suicide is in P'u Sung-ling's story "Li Ssu-chien," P'U 426 (di Giura 337; bowdlerized version in Giles, *Strange Stories*, pp. 212–13). As recounted by P'u, Li Ssu-chien was a *chü-jen* from Yungnien county, arrested for murdering his wife in 1665. As he was being led toward the yamen for trial, Li broke away from his guards, snatched a butcher's knife from a roadside meat stall, ran to the City God's temple, and knelt before the god's image, crying out, "The God blames me for heeding the counsel of worthless men, and for blurring right and wrong with my village cronies. He orders me to cut off an ear." So he severed his left ear and threw it to the ground. And again he cried, "The God blames me for swindling people out of their money. He orders me to cut off a finger." So he cut off one of the fingers on his left hand. And again he cried, "The God blames me for my adulteries with the wives of others, and makes me castrate myself." Li did so, and from that wound he died.

100. Poor women's suicides: These are both listed in the *I-chou chih*: 6/37 is a woman Liu living just north of T'an; according to 6/41 the trader's wife lived just inside T'an jurisdiction. She is a rare case of a woman with a baby committing suicide.

100–101. Another woman Liu: FENG 7/20b.

101. Thirteen-year-old girl: A supplementary biography added to the *lieh-nü chuan* in *T'an-ch'eng hsien-chih* (1763) 10/9, "Wang Shih." In P'u 78 an orphan girl in this situation is raped at the age of nine by her future husband; and in another story in P'u 1283–86, "Ch'iao-nü," P'u gives a moving example of a woman's loyalty to her fiancé.

101. Long memories: Woman Wang's father-in-law will re-appear below; headman Yü, T'an-ch'eng hsien-chih (1763) 9/9b; widow Fan, FENG 7/29b.

102. Women Hsieh and T'ien: FENG 7/22b–23. (I have consistently modified Chinese ages in *sui* to accord with Western usage.)

102. Woman Ho: FENG 7/26b.

102. Woman Ch'en: FENG 7/22b; her husband was the Tu Chih-tung who was killed in 1651. The version of her story in *T'an-ch'eng hsien-chih* (1763) is weakened by cutting graphic details and adding a passage of hortatory dialogue.

102–103. Others survived: Hsü, FENG 7/29; Yang, 7/23b; Kao, 7/28b.

103–104. Chang's wife: P'u 1527–28, "Chang Shih Fu"—this was one of the stories omitted from the Ch'ien-lung published edition of P'u's works. (The second half of the story is omitted here.)

104–105. Scholar Tsung: P'u 682, "Ho hua san-niang-tzu"; di Giura 860.

105. Women's prices: 15 taels, P'u 601 and 1387 (ibid. 1022–1023, 10 nights for 30 taels); 1000, ibid. 709; 200, ibid. 791; 100, ibid. 883; 10, ibid. 423; 3, ibid. 431. See also Susan Naquin, *Millenarian Rebellion,* p. 282, where a woman is priced at ten taels, and an eleven-year-old boy at one tael.

106. P'u on sensuality: Divorces, 1110, 1156; vengeance, 368, 374, 1404; homosexual literati, 317, 1530, 1573; plain women, 642, 1107, 1283; savages, 353; strong women, 1243; illegitimate child, 311; life of virginity, 929 (for Ma-ku's birth in T'an-ch'eng, see Doré, *Recherches* XII, 1118); wit and sex, 1268.

106–107. Woman Yen: P'u 766–69.

107–109. "Tou Shih": P'u 712–14. The story concludes with a long, complex, divine revenge against the callous seducer.

109–116. "Yün Ts'ui-hsien": P'u 748–54; di Giura 1097–1104.

117. Many fewer women: *T'an-ch'eng hsien-chih* (1810) 34–38 gives population figures broken down by sex and child-adult differences; Huang discusses infanticide in HUANG 364d; Yang, *Chinese Village*, p. 10, on low reporting; FENG, chuan 7 for multiple wives of wealthy in the *lieh-nü chuan*.

117. Brought in: *T'an-ch'eng hsien-chih* (1763), describing a different woman Wang.

117. Wang and Jen: These details of their lives can be ascertained from the report in HUANG; i.e., p. 167c, Jen's own testimony on his work; p. 169a, autopsy report on Wang's bound feet; p. 168a, the priest's testimony on the flight story. The date of her flight is calculated by working back from the date of her death, which was late in the twelfth month of K'ang-hsi's tenth year.

117–18. Flight routes: FENG 2/8.

118. P'ei: Water routes from T'an-ch'eng are in FENG 2/8. Natural disasters in P'ei are listed in *P'ei-chou chih* 3/2, 4/17, 5/1, 6/6b. The county capital was moved to a new location, nearer the T'an-ch'eng border, in 1689.

118–19. T'an-ch'eng city: Patrols and questioning travelers, HUANG 359a and b; dishonesty at inns, 127b, with special reference to those coming to town to handle litigation (Huang said such owners were also in league with yamen clerks who would protract the litigation to raise profits); registration at inns, 247b and c; nighttime regulations, 262d–263b. Huang notes how strictly he enforced these *pao-chia* measures in T'an-ch'eng city itself between 1670 and 1672, 215c.

119. Ma-t'ou: Sacked, FENG 9/9b and 7/27 (Yao Shih), and *T'an-ch'eng hsien-chih* (1763) 5/18b; garrison troops were stationed there later on, according to *T'an-ch'eng hsien-chih* (1763) 4/16b, listing eighteen cavalry and sixty infantry; earlier, in the Ming dynasty, there had been a minor tax official there, 7/20b; markets, 4/9b;

temples, festivals, gardens, 4/6–12; doctors, 9/18. General commercial life is described in HUANG 73c–74c.

120. Wife free to leave: Boulais, *Manuel*, p. 300, "Observations."

120. Ning-yang case: Shen Chih-ch'i, *Ta-Ch'ing lü* 19/9b–10; "severing the bonds" is *"shih fu-kang."*

120. Runaway wives: *Tu-li ts'un-i*, p. 312 (clause 116.00.5); Staunton, *Penal Code*, p. 121 (section 116). For other harborers of fugitives, see Staunton, *Penal Code*, pp. 228 and 236 (sections 217 and 223).

120–21. Adultery law: *Tu-li ts'un-i*, p. 1079 (clause 366.00); Staunton, *Penal Code*, pp. 404–405 (section 366); Boulais, *Manuel*, pp. 680–81 (sections 1580–84). The number of blows given in Staunton differs from the other sources here.

121. Husband's revenge: *Tu-li ts'un-i*, p. 783 (clause 285.00); Staunton, *Penal Code*, p. 307 (section 285); Boulais, *Manuel*, pp. 546–47 (sections 1232–35).

121–22. On the road: Humble professions (*yin-yang hsüeh-kuan*), FENG 2/3b. Different professions as listed in Brunnert and Hagelstrom, p. 430 (no. 850). On peddlers, see HUANG 101d; work for fugitives, 214b; prevalence of fugitives, 72d. The very high numbers of Shantung fugitives at this time are also discussed by Fujita Keiichi, "Shinsho Santō," p. 133.

122. Police clerk Wei: HUANG 215c–216b.

123. Confidence games: HUANG 218d–219a.

123. Ferrymen: HUANG 359d–360a, citing the *Wei-hsin pien*.

123–24. Work for women: HUANG 151b, 209a, go-betweens and guarantors; on orphanages and old-folks' homes, 313c and 363c and d (Huang mentions orphanages with up to ninety nurses, but there is unlikely to have been anything on such a scale in T'an-ch'eng); on gambling and brothels set up by gentry, see 269d, 270b. It was not just the fact that the brothels were both morally shameful and a frequent center for the exchange of stolen goods that upset Huang; he argued that after visiting the brothels the post-station riders, in particular, slept in exhaustion till the sun was high, and even as they rode away were still dazed and distracted, 344d–345a.

124. Three Forces: "San-kuan" doctrines summarized in Werner, *Chinese Mythology,* pp. 400–403, and in Stephan Feuchtwang, "Domestic and Communal Worship in Taiwan," pp. 112–13 (in Arthur Wolf, ed., *Religion and Ritual,* pp. 105–29). This seems to have been a small village temple, not one of the three listed in FENG 4/7.

124–25. At the temple: All this dialogue was recorded by Kao in his testimony, HUANG 168a and b.

125–26. Blows: *Tu-li ts'un-i,* p. 889 (clause 302.00); Staunton, *Penal Code,* pp. 324–27 (section 302).

126–27. Divorce law: *Tu-li ts'un-i,* p. 312 (clause 116); Boulais, *Manuel,* pp. 300–303 (sections 633–45); Staunton, *Penal Code,* pp. 120–22 (section 116).

127. Woman Wang's last two months: Huang guesses Jen planned to kill his wife as soon as he got her back, 168d. The new mat figures at intervals in his description of the case. HUANG 294a–c describes the records of good and bad behavior down to the village level.

127. The cold: Huang's account shows it was snowing. Mean temperatures are in Bell, pp. 45, 46, and 53, and in Buck, *Statistics,* table V, p. 7. Poor Shantung homes are carefully described in Yang, *Chinese Village,* pp. 38–40.

127–28. The quarrel: HUANG 168d.

128. Her clothes: HUANG 169a.

128. Winter lake: P'u 580.

128. Winter mountains: P'u 1261.

128. The room: P'u 150.

128. The blossoms: P'u 439–40.

128. Face and hands: P'u 294, 282.

128. Her smile: P'u 1182, 1433.

128. Sleeping place: P'u 1280–81.

129. Massage: P'u 637, 1001, 774, 908.

129. Tumor: P'u 60–61.

129. Tired: P'u 1268.

129. Her retainers: P'u 647.

129. Doors: P'u 394.

129. Courtyard and swing: P'u 647–48.

129. The boat: P'u 706.

129. The wind: P'u 1261.

130. Clouds and stars: P'u 416.
130. The steps: P'u 342.
130. Fruit and wine: P'u 300.
130. Peonies and camellias: P'u 1548.
130. Unknown instrument: P'u 947.
130. Sings of the women: P'u 59.
130. Breeze and birds: P'u 985.
130. The tree, the bird: P'u 460.
130. Shoes and dew: P'u 535, 538.
130. The tower: P'u 1525–26.
131. He trembles: P'u 855.
131. Food and night soil: P'u 861–62.
131. Embroidered shoes: P'u 1588.
131. Woman's cap: P'u 724.
131. Make-up and cotton football: P'u 1001.
131. Transparent ball: P'u 371.
131. The tower vanishes: P'u 1526.
131. The snot, the lady: P'u 122.
131. Mouth full of earth: P'u 1535.
131. The snake: P'u 172, 579.
131. The water, the people: P'u 585.
131–32. The death: Huang Liu-hung's autopsy report, HUANG 169d.
132. Jen's story: HUANG 167c and d.
132. The body: HUANG 169a.

EPILOGUE: THE TRIAL

133. The first day: HUANG 167c and d. Huang presents this orally, to heighten the effect of what he calls his "chuan-ch'i" style of recitation, but I am assuming he was summarizing the original deposition.
133–34. Procedures: Scribes and depositions, HUANG 49, 120a; Sealed depositions, 119–121; temporary warrants, 123c–124a; city prison, FENG maps, and 2/4.
134. Prison: Abuses, HUANG 151a–152c (Bodde, "Prison Life," has dramatic confirmation of similar conditions, drawn from Fang Pao's experiences in 1712–1713); amelioration, 152d–153a, 154; organization, 153.

135–36. The second day: HUANG 167c–168c; trial procedures, 128b–129c; investigation procedures, 130.

136–37. The third day: HUANG 168c–169c; autopsy procedures, 164, 173–75.

137. City God: Used by Huang to awe local headmen in charge of tax collection, HUANG 109a and b. P'u Sungling has a magistrate use the City God's temple for similar purposes in the story "Yen-chih," P'u 1373.

137–39. The fourth day: HUANG 169c–170d; death from beatings, 40c and 53c; use of cangue, 131c.

139. Hungry ghosts: Woman T'ien, FENG 7/24b; Ahern, *Cult of the Dead*, pp. 241–44; Jordan, *Gods, Ghosts and Ancestors*, pp. 33–36; Huang on her shade, 170a, and three-tael reward to family of deceased, 53; on this other occasion the family were also given a tax exemption of one *ting*.

Bibliography

AHERN, EMILY. *The Cult of the Dead in a Chinese Village*. Stanford: Stanford University Press, 1973.

BELL, MARK A. *China: Being a Military Report on the Northeastern Portions of the Provinces of Chih-li and Shan-tung; Nanking and its Approaches; Canton and its Approaches; etc., etc.* 2 vols. Simla: Government Central Branch Press, 1884.

BISHOP, JOHN LYMAN. *The Colloquial Short Story in China: A Study of the San-yen Collections*. Cambridge, Mass.: Harvard University Press, 1956.

BODDE, DERK. "Prison Life in Eighteenth-Century Peking." *Journal of the American Oriental Society*, 89 (1969): 311–33.

———— AND MORRIS, CLARENCE. *Law in Imperial China, Exemplified by 190 Ch'ing Dynasty Cases*. Cambridge, Mass.: Harvard University Press, 1967.

BOULAIS, GUY. *Manuel du code chinois*. Variétés sinologiques, no. 55. Shanghai, 1924.

BRUNNERT, H. S., AND HAGELSTROM, V. V. *Present Day Political Organization of China*. Translated by A. Beltchenko and E. E. Moran. Shanghai: Kelly and Walsh, 1911.

BUCK, DAVID D. "The Provincial Elite in Shantung during the Republican Period: Their Successes and Failures." *Modern China*, 1:4 (October 1975): 417–46.

BUCK, JOHN LOSSING. *Land Utilization in China: A Study of 16,786 Farms in 168 Localities. . . . II: Statistics. III: Atlas*. Nanking: University of Nanking Press, 1937.

CHAN HOK-LAM. "The White Lotus-Maitreya Doctrine and Popular Uprisings in Ming and Ch'ing China." *Sinologica*, Separatum Volume 10 (1969): 211–33.

CHANG CHING-CH'IAO 張景樵. *"Liao-chai chih-i" yüan-kao k'ao-cheng* 聊齋志異原稿考證 [A Study of the Original Draft Manuscript of the *Liao-chai chih-i*]. Taipei, 1968.

CHANG CHUN-SHU AND CHANG HSÜEH-LUN. "The World of P'u

163

Sung-ling's *Liao-chai chih-i:* Literature and the Intelligentsia during the Ming-Ch'ing Dynastic Transition," *Journal of the Institute of Chinese Studies* (Chinese University of Hong Kong), 6:2 (1973): 401–23.

CHANG P'EI 章 沛. *"Liao-chai chih-i ko pieh tso-p'in chung-ti min-tsu ssu-hsiang"* 聊齋志異個別作品中的民族思想 [Nationalist Thought in the *Liao-chai chih-i*]. *Wen-hsüeh i-ch'an tseng-k'an* 文學遺產增刊, no. 6 (1958): 269–80.

CHANG YAO 張 曜. *Shan-tung chün-hsing chi-lüeh* 山東軍興紀畧 [History of Military Campaigns in Shantung]. 22 chuan. Taipei: Wen-hai ch'u-pan-she reprint, n.d.

CHAO MENG-AN 禚夢庵. "T'an-ch'eng I-nan shih-she" 郯城沂南詩社 [The I River Poetry Club of T'an-ch'eng]. *Shan-tung wen-hsien* 山東文獻, 2:4 (1977): 57–58.

CH'EN WAN-NAI 陳萬鼐. *Hung Sheng yen-chiu* 洪昇研究 [A Study of Hung Sheng]. Taipei: Taiwan Hsüeh-sheng shu-chü, 1970.

CH'ENG CHENG-K'UEI 程正揆. *Ts'ang-chou chi-shih* 滄洲紀事 [Memoir of the Ts'ang-chou Area in 1644]. In *Ch'ing-t'o i-shih* 荊駝逸史, ts'e 32.

CHENG T'IEN-T'ING et al. 鄭天挺. *Ming-mo nung-min ch'i-i shih-liao* 明末農民起義史料 [Materials on the Late Ming Peasant Uprisings]. Peking, 1952.

CHING SU AND LO LUN 景甦、羅崙. *Ch'ing-tai Shan-tung ching-ying ti-chu ti she-hui hsing-chih* 清代山東經營地主底社會性質 [Social Characteristics of Shantung Managerial Landlords during the Ch'ing]. Shantung: Jen-min ch'u-pan she, 1959.

CHU, YUNG-DEH RICHARD. "An Introductory Study of the White Lotus Sect in Chinese History with Special Reference to Peasant Movements." Ph.D. dissertation, Columbia University, 1967.

DI GIURA, LUDOVICO NICOLA, trans. *I Racconti Fantastici di Liao* [translation of P'u Sung-ling's *Liao-chai chih-i*]. Milan: Arnoldo Mondadori [1926], 1962.

DORÉ, HENRI. *Recherches sur les superstitions en Chine.* Variétés sinologiques, no. 48: *Le panthéon chinois* (fin); Variétés sinologiques, no. 49: *Popularisation du confucéisme.* . . . Shanghai: Imprimerie de la Mission Catholique, 1918.

DUNSTAN, HELEN. "The Late Ming Epidemics: A Preliminary Survey." *Ch'ing-shih wen-t'i*, 3:3 (1975): 1–59.

EBERHARD, WOLFRAM. *Chinesische Träume und ihre Deutung.* Akademie der Wissenschaften und der Literatur, Abhandlungen der

Geistes und Sozialwissenschaftlichen Klasse, Jahrgang 1974, nr. 14. Wiesbaden: Franz Steiner Verlag, 1971.

FA-SHIH-SHAN 法式善. *Ch'ing-pi shu-wen* 清秘述聞 [Examiners and Examination Questions in the Early Ch'ing]. 16 chuan, 1798. Taipei: Wen-hai ch'u-pan-she reprint, n.d.

FENG K'O-TS'AN. See note on p. 141.

Fu-hui ch'üan-shu, 1694. See note on p. 141.

FUJITA KEIICHI 藤田敬一. "Shinsho Santō ni okeru fuekisei ni tsuite" 清初山東に おけろ 賦役制に ついて [The Tax and Corvée System in Shantung during the Early Ch'ing Period]. *Tōyōshi kenkyū* 東洋史研究, 24:2 (September 1965): 127–51.

GILES, HERBERT A., trans. *Strange Stories from a Chinese Studio.* Rev. ed. London: T. W. Laurie, 1916.

Hai-chou chih-li-chou chih 海州直隸州志 [Gazetteer of the Independent Department of Hai-chou]. 32 chuan. 1811. Taipei: Ch'en-wen reprint, 1970.

HERVOUET, YVES, general editor. *Contes extraordinaires du pavillon du loisir, par P'ou Song-ling.* Collection UNESCO d'oeuvres representatives, 31. Serie chinoise. Paris: Gallimard, 1969.

HIGHTOWER, JAMES ROBERT. *Topics in Chinese Literature, Outlines and Bibliographies.* Cambridge, Mass.: Harvard University Press, 1962.

HO MAN-TZU 何滿子. *P'u Sung-ling yü "Liao-chai chih-i"* 蒲松齡與聊齋誌異 [A Study of P'u Sung-ling's *Liao-chai chih-i*]. Shanghai, 1965.

HO PING-TI. *Studies on the Population of China, 1368–1953.* Cambridge, Mass.: Harvard University Press, 1959.

HSIAO KUNG-CHUAN. *Rural China: Imperial Control in the Nineteenth Century.* Seattle: University of Washington Press, 1960.

HSIEH KUO-CHEN 謝國楨. *Ch'ing-ch'u nung-min ch'i-i tzu-liao chi-lu* 清初農民起義資料輯錄 [Sources on Peasant Risings in the Early Ch'ing]. Shanghai, 1956.

HUANG LIU-HUNG. See note on p. 141.

HUANG, RAY. *Taxation and Governmental Finance in Sixteenth-Century Ming China.* Cambridge: Cambridge University Press, 1974.

Hui-tien shih-li 會典事例 [Ch'ing Statutes and Precedents]. Taipei: Ch'i-wen ch'u-pan she reprint, 1963.

HUMMEL, ARTHUR, ed. *Eminent Chinese of the Ch'ing Period,* 2 vols. Washington, D.C., 1943–44.

I-chou chih 沂州志 [Gazetteer of I-chou]. 8 chuan. 1674.

I-chou fu-chih 沂州府志 [Gazetteer of I-chou]. 36 chuan. 1760.

I hsien-chih 嶧縣志 [Gazetteer of I County]. 10 chuan. 1761.

IRWIN, RICHARD GREGG. *The Evolution of a Chinese Novel: Shui-hu-chuan*. Cambridge, Mass.: Harvard University Press, 1966.

JORDAN, DAVID K. *Gods, Ghosts, and Ancestors: The Folk Religion of a Taiwanese Village*. Berkeley: University of California Press, 1972.

(Ts'ao-chou fu) Ko-tse hsien hsiang-t'u chih 曹州府菏澤縣鄉土志 [Gazetteer of Ko-tse County]. 1 chuan. 1908. Taipei: Ch'eng-wen reprint, 1968.

LADSTÄTTER, OTTO. "P'u Sung-ling und seine Werke in Umgangssprache." Inaugural dissertation, Ludwig-Maximilians University, Munich, 1960.

Lai-yang hsien-chih 萊陽縣志 [Gazetteer of Lai-yang]. 34 chuan. 1935.

LEGGE, JAMES. *The Chinese Classics*. 5 vols. Rev. ed. Oxford: Clarendon Press, 1893–1895.

LI WEN-CHIH 李文治. *Wan-Ming min-pien* 晚明民變 [Popular Uprisings in the Late Ming]. Hong Kong: Yuan-tung t'u-shu kung-ssu reprint, 1966.

LI YÜ 李漁. *Tzu-chih hsin-shu* 資治新書 [Collected Essays on Administration]. 14 chuan, 1663; 20 chuan, 1667.

Liao-chai chih-i. See note on p. 141.

Lin-i hsien-chih 臨沂縣志 [Gazetteer of Lin-i]. 14 chuan. 1916.

LIU CHIEH-P'ING 劉階平. *Liao-chai pien-nien shih-chi hsüan-chu* 聊齋編年詩集選注 [Poems of P'u Sung-ling, Chronologically Arranged and Annotated]. Taipei: Chung-hua Shu-chü, 1974.

LU TA-HUAN 路大荒. "P'u Liu-yüan hsien-sheng nien-p'u" 蒲柳泉先生年譜 [A Chronological Biography of P'u Sung-ling], in *P'u Sung-ling chi*, pp. 1745–1801.

METZGER, THOMAS. *The Internal Organization of Ch'ing Bureaucracy: Legal, Normative, and Communication Aspects*. Cambridge, Mass.: Harvard University Press, 1973.

MYERS, RAMON H. "Commercialization, Agricultural Development, and Landlord Behavior in Shantung Province in the Late Ch'ing Period." *Ch'ing-shih wen-t'i*, 2:8 (May 1972): 31–55.

NAKAMURA JIHEI 中村治兵衛. "Shindai Santō no gakuden" 清代山東の學田 [Shantung School Lands during the Ch'ing Dynasty]. *Shien* 史淵, 64 (February 1955): 43–63.

————. "Shindai Santō no gakuden no kosaku" 清代山東の學田 の小作 [Tenancy on Shantung School Lands during the Ch'ing Dynasty]. *Shien* 史淵, 71 (December 1956): 55–77.

NISHIMURA GENSHO 西村元照. "Shinsho no tochi jōryō ni tsuite" 清初の土地丈量について [Land Surveys in the Early Ch'ing Period]. *Tōyōshi-kenkyū* 東洋史研究 33:3 (December 1974): 102–55.

Pa-ch'i t'ung-chih 八旗通志 [History of the Eight Banners]. 1739 ed. Taipei: Hsüeh-sheng shu-chü reprint, 1968.

P'AN SHAO-TS'AN 潘杓燦. *Wei-hsin pien* 未信編 [Treatise on Local Administration]. 6 chuan. 1684.

P'ei-chou chih 邳州志 [Gazetteer of P'ei-chou]. 20 chuan. 1851 ed. Taipei: Ch'eng-wen reprint, 1970.

P'ENG SUN-I 彭孫貽. *P'ing-k'ou chih* 平寇志 [Account of Rebel Pacifications, 1628–1661]. 12 chuan. 1931 ed.

Pi hsien-chih 費縣志 [Gazetteer of Pi (Fei) County]. 10 chuan. 1689.

(*Hsü-hsiu*) *Po-shan hsien-chih* 續修博山縣志 [Further Continuation of the Po-shan Gazetteer]. 15 chuan. 1937. Taipei: Ch'eng-wen reprint, 1968.

PRUŠEK, JAROSLAV. *Chinese History and Literature: Collection of Studies*. Dordrecht: D. Reidel, 1970.

P'U SUNG-LING. See note on p. 141.

————. *Liao-chai chih-i,* translations from. See Di Giura, Giles, Hervouet, Quong.

P'u Sung-ling chi 蒲松齡集 [Collected Works of P'u Sung-ling— Essays, Poems, Plays]. 2 vols. Shanghai: Chung-hua shu-chü, 1962.

P'u Sung-ling yen-chiu tzu-liao 蒲松齡研究資料 [Collected Studies on P'u Sung-ling]. 2 vols. Hong Kong: T'ao-chai shu-wu, 1974.

QUONG, ROSE, trans. *Chinese Ghost and Love Stories: A Selection from the Liao Chai Stories by P'u Sung-ling*. New York: Pantheon, 1946.

Shan-tung ti-fang-shih chiang-shou t'i-kang 山東地方史講授提綱 [Discussion of Major Themes in the Local History of Shantung]. Chinan: Shantung Jen-min ch'u-pan-she, 1960.

Shan-tung t'ung-chih 山東通志 [Gazetteer of Shantung Province]. 64 chuan. 1678.

————. 200 chuan. 1911.

(*Chung-tsuan*) *Shao-wu fu-chih* 重纂邵武府志 [Complete Gazetteer of Shao-wu Prefecture]. 30 chuan. 1900. Taipei: Ch'eng-wen ch'u-pan-she reprint, 1967.

Shao-wu-fu hsü-chih 邵武府續志 [Continuation of the Shao-wu Gazetteer]. 10 chuan. 1670.

SHEN CHIH-CH'I 沈之奇. *Ta-ch'ing lü chi-chu* 大清律輯註 [Commentary on the Ch'ing Legal Code]. 30 chuan (1715). 1755 ed.

Shih-lu 實 錄 [Veritable Records of the Ch'ing Dynasty, Arranged by Reign]. Taipei: Hua-wen shu-chü reprint, 1964.

SHRYOCK, JOHN. *The Temples of Anking and Their Cults: A Study of Modern Chinese Religion.* Paris: Geuthner, 1931.

STAUNTON, SIR GEORGE. *Ta Tsing Leu Lee; Being the Fundamental Laws . . . of the Penal Code of China.* London, 1810; reprint ed., Taipei: Ch'eng-wen, 1966.

Su-ch'ien hsien-chih 宿遷縣志 [Gazetteer of Su-ch'ien hsien]. 19 chuan. 1875; reprint, 1965.

SUN T'ING-CH'ÜAN 孫廷銓. *Yen-shan tsa-chi* 顏山雜記. 4 chuan. 1665.

T'an-ch'eng hsien-chih, 1673. See note on p. 141.

(Chung-hsiu) T'an-ch'eng hsien-chih 重修郯城縣志 [Continuation of the T'an-ch'eng Gazetteer]. 12 chuan. 1763.

(Hsü-hsiu) T'an-ch'eng hsien-chih 續修郯城縣志 [Further Continuation of the T'an-ch'eng Gazetteer]. 10 chuan. 1810; reprint ed., Taipei: Ch'eng-wen ch'u-pan-she, 1968.

T'an-ch'eng hsien fu-i ch'üan-shu 郯城縣賦役全書 [Complete Tax and Labor Service of T'an-ch'eng]. 1 chuan, 1897.

T'AN CH'IEN 談 遷. *Kuo-chüeh* 國 榷 [History of the Ming Dynasty]. Completed by 1655. 6 vols. Peking, 1958.

T'eng hsien-chih 滕縣志 [Gazetteer of T'eng County]. 14 chuan. 1832.

Tsou hsien-chih 鄒縣志 [Gazetteer of Tsou County]. 3 chuan. 1716.

Tu-li ts'un-i 讀例存疑. By Hsüeh Yün-sheng 薛允升 [Analysis of Problems in the Legal Code]. Edited by Huang Tsing-chia 黃靜嘉. 5 vols. Taipei: Ch'eng-wen ch'u-pan-she, 1970.

Tung-kuang hsien-chih 東光縣志 [Gazetteer of Tung-kuang County]. 8 chuan. 1693

Tzu-ch'uan hsien-chih 淄川縣志 [Gazetteer of Tzu-ch'uan]. 8 chuan. 1743.

WANG CHIH 王 植. "T'an-ch'eng Yin Huang Ssu-hu chuan" 郯城尹黃思湖傳 [Biography of the T'an-ch'eng Magistrate Huang Liu-hung]. In *Chung-te-t'ang kao* 崇德堂藁, chuan 4.

WANG YEH-CHIEN. *Land Taxation in Imperial China, 1750–1911.* Cambridge, Mass.: Harvard University Press, 1973.

WOLF, ARTHUR P., ed. *Religion and Ritual in Chinese Society.* Stanford: Stanford University Press, 1974.

YAMANE YUKIO. See note on p. 141, under Huang.

YANG JEN-K'AI 楊仁愷. "*Liao-chai chih-i*" *yüan-kao yen-chiu* 聊齋志異原稿研究 [A Study of the Original Draft Manuscript of the *Liao-chai chih-i*]. Shenyang, 1958.

YANG LIU 楊 柳. "*Liao-chai chih-i*" *yen-chiu* 聊齋志異研究 [A Study of the *Liao-chai chih-i*]. Nanking, 1958.

YANG, MARTIN C. *A Chinese Village: Taitou, Shantung Province.* New York: Columbia University Press, 1945; paperback, 1965.

YOKOYAMA SUGURU 橫山英. "Kampōki Santō no kōryō fūchō to mindan" 咸豐期山東の抗糧風潮と民團 [Popular Organizations and Peasant Uprisings in Protest against High Rents and Taxes during the Hsien-feng Reign in Shantung]. *Rekishi kyōiku* 歷史教育, new series 12:9 (September 1964): 42–50.